TURNING PEOPLE ON

The Motivation Challenge

About the Author

Andrew Sargent started work as a Civil Servant in the East End of London. Later, he became a Personnel Manager with the Union International Company before joining the Industrial Society – initially as a Management and Training Adviser, and then as Communication and Industrial Relations Director. He joined the CBI to run its Employee Communication and Involvement advisory service, and to advise on its own campaign for voluntary employee participation and involvement in British organizations. In 1978 he started his own management consultancy company, Sargent Minton Lennon Ltd, which specializes in the introduction and management of organizational change.

He believes vehemently that business success and the enthusiasm and motivation of workpeople are linked together. For this link to be effective, however, personnel specialists must be prepared to be measured by bottom-line results. *Turning People On* is the result of his own experience.

Andrew Sargent is the author of *The Missing Workforce: Managing Absenteeism,* also published by the IPM. He lives in Leigh on Sea with his wife Rhiannon. He has two children.

TURNING PEOPLE ON

The Motivation Challenge

Andrew Sargent

Institute of Personnel Management

Phototypeset by James Jenkins Typesetting, London
and printed in Great Britain by
Short Run Press Ltd., Exeter, Devon

British Library Cataloguing in Publication Data
Sargent, Andrew
    Turning people on
    1.   Personnel. Motivation. Management
    I.   Title
    658.314

    ISBN 0-85292-444-5

The views expressed in this book are the author's own, and may not necessarily reflect those of the IPM.

For Rhiannon
and for
my mother and father

'How beauteous mankind is. O brave
new world that has such people in't'
The Tempest

Contents

Acknowledgements

I am grateful to Trevor Day, Roger Moores and Colin Minton for their help in putting this book together. Daphne Smith and Teresa Little did the typing – my thanks, as ever, to them.

Dennis Ruabon Ltd and Tinsley Bridge Ltd both kindly agreed to be written about in some detail. I'm proud to be associated with them and acknowledge their help. I also thank Tesco Stores for allowing me to use their communication policy and the other organizations who supplied examples, although, for obvious reasons, I haven't named them all.

Finally, I'm grateful to have been given the opportunity by IPM of writing all this down. I hope they find it all as worthwile.

Author's Note

Dear Personnel Manager,

I earn my living as a management consultant and many of my principal points of contact are people like you. One of the things that frustrates them is their inability really to influence policy in their own organizations – so they have to employ people like me to say what they claim to have been recommending for years!

This book sets out my experience of the initiatives you can take to influence the way in which people are managed. I haven't recommended anything that doesn't work, although you obviously need to tailor my suggestions to the particular needs of your organization. I hope you'll find at least some of them useful.

Andrew Sargent

Chapter 1
The Challenge

Sometimes one wonders whether we've learned anything new about employee relations in the last decade. Consider, for example, a current panacea: share option schemes. It cannot make sense to expect employees to have no (or very little) say in the affairs of their companies and, at the same time, to invest their savings as well as their working lives in the very enterprise that could make them redundant ('Very sorry, chaps, but owing to interest rates you're all out of a job. We can't sell our products in the marketplace. You can sell your shares, of course – but they're not worth anything at the moment, so really you should hang on').

Whether people decide to invest their money in this way is, of course, a matter for them. But it is naive to think that buying a few shares in an enterprise whose policy you cannot in any way influence is going to make people feel any more involved, committed or participative. And certainly it isn't what motivation is about. There's far more to it than that.

Yet what employers and employees want and expect of each other is much more deliverable than many observers would think. To support such an assertion, let us address a few facts.

First, most people would rather win than lose. They would rather contribute towards the attainment of realistic objectives than simply stand or sit around like pawns, while the kings, queens and knights make all the moves. They already *are* involved. Simply turning up for work guarantees that. What they want – and what their employers need them to do – is to play a constructive part. That means joining in – or, if you prefer, participating.

In order for people to join in, there must be a structure which enables them to do so. Some leading organizations have achieved great and lasting change by encouraging employees to participate in their businesses. It may have meant abandoning a few 'principles', such as 'Only I have the right to manage', but at the end of the day it's been the means of succeeding. Ask British Airways how much

1

change and prosperity would have been possible without the participation of the British Airways Trade Union Council. Ask ICI whether it would like to disband its sophisticated and well-ordered hierarchy of employee representative committees, or Cadbury Schweppes or Rowntrees. Or many more.

> When a leading Japanese automotive manufacturer opened discussions with a British plant about a possible joint venture, the Japanese asked for information about the structure of the organization. Various charts were produced or hastily drawn up to illustrate how everything worked, and what the various reporting relationships were.
> The Japanese watched all this with interest and one of them, finally, asked: 'British company structure like Army?'
> 'Well, yes, if you put it like that.'
> 'Ah! Japanese company structured like manufacturer!'

For the enormous majority of organizations – or, at least, prosperous organizations – employee involvement has meant employee commitment. For most employees, having a seat on the board is irrelevant. Yet, the chance to learn more about the business, to put ideas forward and see them implemented has created a greater sense of belonging than any share option scheme ever achieved. Why does government and its policy advisers, whether current or past, think loyalty can always be bought?

There is now an opportunity to get it right at long last. Does anybody really think that Britain will be allowed by its European colleagues to enter the post-1992 era *and continue* to pour scorn on Europe's values and beliefs? Why, for example, is it that involvement is second nature to the Germans (and Japanese) – and considered by us to be some kind of optional extra?

The Personnel Manager's Role

This is primarily a book for personnel specialists, but also for line managers. I profoundly believe that the potential is vast for personnel managers to influence the way people are managed at work, yet that potential is not exploited at all in many industries and organizations. The fact of the matter is that millions of managers are crying out for help with their 'people' responsibilities. Personnel management, if it is to survive and flourish, needs to become enormously more initiatory in this regard.

Chapter 2
What the Behavioural Scientists Say

Mid-afternoon in an outdoor factory site somewhere in the West Midlands. It is early February, the ground is frozen and Dave's breath is freezing to his collar. He's been at his job all day. He rolls another gas cylinder into place, applies the nozzle and clamp, and the pressure rises slowly towards 120 p.s.i. He moves the lever back, disconnects the hose, rolls the cylinder away to the rack of over a hundred he's done earlier in the day, and rolls another into place. Dave is on the outdoor shift for one week. Next week he'll be indoors, filling cylinders inside the depot.

Julia looks at her watch and thinks: 'It's ten minutes past five, and this bloody meeting is going on for ages – a waste of time.' She looks at the male, middle-aged faces around the boardroom table. They show various expressions ranging from inspirational excitement – the present speaker, John, is expounding on his pet topic, 'the management of change' – to the bored, quizzical and finally, glazed-over. Julia thinks of her husband, who will be shortly picking up the two children from the minder after work. 'There's got to be an easier way of earning a living,' she thinks to herself as she shuffles her feet and plans her strategy for leaving the meeting early.

What's all this got to do with motivation? What indeed? I asked myself the same question after I left the Quality Assurance Manager's office at a major manufacturing firm and then descended to the factory floor. The spotlessly clean, luxurious office I left behind was in total contrast to the sticky, black layer of grime that covered everything, including the people, in the rubber compound mixing room.

It is easy to talk about theories of motivation and to get an intellectual sense of what they mean. It is quite another to see how such theories can be applied in practice by managers and supervisors. So let us not only look at the spotlessly clean intellectual walls of the behavioural psychologists but also at how their ideas can be applied in practice – to people like Dave and Julia, for example.

3

Motivation and Commitment

Motivation is about what makes people tick, what makes people act
or behave in particular ways. On a basic level, people are motivated
towards a desired outcome, such as congratulations from their
manager for a job well done, or are motivated to *avoid* an undesired
outcome, such as a rollicking from the boss for work being late.

We are not automatons. Our motives for behaving the way we do
are many and varied. Take Julia, for example. Whether she stays
behind at work to finish a report for her senior manager will depend
on a whole complex of variables: her prediction as to what will
happen if she doesn't finish the report today; what her mental state
is at the time – exhausted or fired with enthusiasm; what arrangements she has made with her husband and children, and so on and
so on.

Many times a day, consciously and unconsciously, we are making
decisions – calculations – as to where to invest our energy. Some of
the factors which affect this calculation lie outside the individual –
they are *extrinsic*. They include, in Julia's case, the pressure from
her boss and commitments at home. Other factors lie within the
individual – they are *intrinsic* – such as how Julia *feels* about the
pressure from her boss and commitments at home, and how she views
herself as an employee and as a family member and contributor. Of
course, extrinsic and intrinsic factors are not clearly separated from
one another, there is a complex interplay between them.

The important point is that extrinsic factors affect the way people
feel about themselves. How an individual like Julia reacts to her
senior manager will be in part a function of the trust and mutual
respect built up between them. As a manager, you have some
control over the extrinsic factors which affect your employees. Over
time, these will influence the way your employees respond to you.
Your history of communication with them and resultant actions
taken will contribute to their commitment, or otherwise, towards
you. In their calculations – taken consciously or unconsciously many
times a day – they will err on your side or not, at least partly as a
result of how they have been treated by you in the past.

Since we are in the business of generating commitment – of
getting people to opt in rather than opt out when they do their
calculations – we need to begin to understand motivation and the
factors that affect it. Let us see what the psychologists and management theorists have to say.

Intrinsic Theories and Motivation

The ideas of Abraham Maslow, a humanistic psychologist, have had a considerable influence on management thinking since the late 1940s. Like Carl Rogers, another humanistic thinker, Maslow had a positive view of human nature, a belief in the individual's potential for personal growth – what they called *self-actualization.*

One of Maslow's great contributions was his *Hierarchy of Needs,* which sees people as having a set of needs which they are motivated to satisfy. These form a hierarchy which can be displayed visually as a pyramid (Figure 1).

Figure 1

Maslow's Hierarchy of Needs

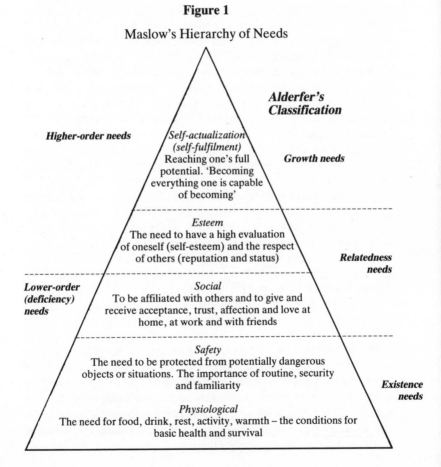

Alderfer's Classification

Higher-order needs

Self-actualization (self-fulfilment)
Reaching one's full potential. 'Becoming everything one is capable of becoming'

Growth needs

Esteem
The need to have a high evaluation of oneself (self-esteem) and the respect of others (reputation and status)

Relatedness needs

Lower-order (deficiency) needs

Social
To be affiliated with others and to give and receive acceptance, trust, affection and love at home, at work and with friends

Safety
The need to be protected from potentially dangerous objects or situations. The importance of routine, security and familiarity

Existence needs

Physiological
The need for food, drink, rest, activity, warmth – the conditions for basic health and survival

Maslow suggested that needs only motivate people when they are unsatisfied. When applied to his hierarchy, *lower-order needs* (basic physical needs, comfort, safety and security) have to be satisfied before *higher-order needs* (self-esteem and personal growth) assert themselves.

How does this apply in practice? If your stomach is protesting loudly that you need food, then you're likely to find reading this book a real struggle. Your lower-order physiological needs are asserting themselves. If you are hungry, your needs for self-development temporarily take a back seat.

OK, but how does this apply to the workplace? If we make sure our workforce is getting its basic physical and safety needs met (reasonable working conditions, job security, etc), what will this mean? Will it mean that employees will now be ready and willing to work with colleagues to meet corporate objectives? Clearly life is not as simple as this. Applying Maslow's model, employees are likely to work towards company goals only where these are in harmony with their own personal goals. Also, following the hierarchy to its logical conclusion, once a certain set of needs are met, the next level will be activated. Employees will never be satisfied until they have scaled the heights of the hierarchy!

There are, of course, many exceptions to the idea of orderly progression up the hierarchy. The starving artist in his garret might be an example, who gives up some of his basic needs – food, safety and security – in the pursuit of creativity.

To be fair to Maslow, he didn't intend that his ideas, which were originally based on observations of clients, should be hijacked by management theorists. Maslow's ideas do lead to an important point, however: in prosperous societies where there is relatively full employment, self-actualization is likely to be a key motivator for at least some people. However, whether people 'self-actualize' at home or at work is another matter entirely. I'm sure we can all think of people who hide their light under a bushel at work, and yet spend their spare time running a local club, making high-precision model trains, or sitting on the local council.

There can't be many working environments where self-actualization is actively encouraged – in research departments, possibly, or some humanistically inclined leading-edge consultancy firms. For most of us, if we choose to, we have to carve out opportunities for self-actualization at work in spite of the prevailing work climate. As one manager put it to me recently, 'Creative thinking is all right in theory – but it doesn't half rock the boat.'

Various researchers have followed up on Maslow's ideas as they apply in the workplace. Fred Herzberg's *two-factor theory* is based on looking at the main factors which result in either satisfying or dissatisfying experiences at work. The assumption is that if the individual is satisfied in their work, that this will mean good performance or, at the very least, a willingness to stay on the job.

Factors leading to dissatisfaction were found to do with conditions of work – company policy and administration, technical supervision, salary, interpersonal relations and physical working conditions. Herzberg called these the *'hygiene'* or *'maintenance'* factors. They are a necessary minimum for a healthy workplace – they may make people come into work and stay there, but they don't necessarily encourage people to be productive. It is the other factors, the *'satisfiers'* or *'motivators'* – achievement, recognition, the work itself, responsibility, advancement – that encourage people to work harder. Interpreted in Maslow's terms, hygiene factors allow us to satisfy our basic needs and avoid pain, while motivators reflect people's need for esteem and self-fulfilment.

A number of researchers have criticized Herzberg's work on various grounds, not least because it was largely based on research with accountants and engineers, so the findings may not apply to shop-floor employees or clerical staff. It is easy to think of a situation where environmental factors *could* lead to greater productivity. For example, in a climate where you have conscientious employees and a keen and concerned manager, peer pressure could create conditions where all or most employees toe the line.

To return to Maslow's hierarchy (and Figure 1), a number of workers have modified his ideas. Alderfer, for example, developed a model – his *ERG theory* – which places individual needs in three groups:

1. *Existence:* the need for basic physiological and material requirements. These include food and shelter and, at work, reasonable pay and working conditions.
2. *Relatedness:* the need for sharing thoughts and feelings. These are met through relationships with family and friends and, at work, with colleagues and supervisors.
3. *Growth:* the need to develop whatever abilities and capacities the individual feels are most important.

Unlike Maslow's hierarchy, Alderfer's checklist of needs operates in either direction. For example, if fulfilment of growth needs is thwarted, individuals concentrate on fulfilling their relatedness needs. Unsatisfied needs, therefore, become less rather than more important, whereas Maslow assumed the opposite. Alderfer's ideas are backed up by some more recent research which shows that relatedness or growth needs actually become more important when satisfied. This means, for example, that team working arrangements which satisfy relatedness needs can continue to motivate employees and are not necessarily superseded by growth needs.

David McClelland and various colleagues identified three types of need as being important in the motivation of managers:

1. The need for *achievement,* defined as the need for competitive success.
2. The need for *affiliation,* defined as the need for warm, friendly relationships with others.
3. The need for *power,* defined as the need to control or influence others.

Using these categories, they discovered that most managers require all three to be met, although to differing extents in different individuals. Yet the need for achievement is well developed in the majority of well-rounded managers.

If these variations in what motivates people also exist among employees, then no single, simple strategy is likely to be successful in motivating everyone. Some, who have a high achievement need, will respond to greater personal responsibility, selecting production targets, moderate goals, and rapid feedback of results. For those with strong affiliation needs this strategy is unlikely to be so successful.

Despite criticisms of the ideas of Maslow, Herzberg and Alderfer, their notion of a 'self-actualizing' or growth need has had considerable influence on management theory and, to an extent, on management practice. Before these theories were popularized there were two models on which management theory and practice could be based: *rational-economic* and *social* man (and presumably 'woman'). The former would expend effort to the extent that it was in his or her economic interest to do so. The latter searched for affiliation and supportive relationships in the workplace, so effort was significantly influenced by the collective work-rate. The notion of self-actualizing man brings in the idea that the individual is primarily self-motivated and, given half a chance, will seek to become mature and competent in the workplace.

One notable attempt to show the connection between different models of motivation and managerial practice was made by Douglas

McGregor in his book *The Human Side of Enterprise* (1960). His premise was that effective leadership depended upon a manager's assumptions about the nature of management and people in general.

McGregor put forward two sets of assumptions about people: *Theory X and Theory Y*. Which set of assumptions you hold in a given situation will influence your behaviour and the way you interact with your employees. You will exert an influence through the content of your speech, tone, gesture, written communication, in fact all forms of communication between you and them.

Theory X is a managerial philosophy which sees employees as basically disliking work, avoiding responsibility, generally unambitious and needing to be coerced, controlled and directed. In other words, it treats them as rational-economic beings requiring either reward or coercion to motivate them. Autocratic managerial styles are the logical result of translating Theory X into management practice.

Theory Y, on the other hand, sees people as *not* by nature passive or resistant to organizational needs. Rather, they have become that way as a result of experience within organizations. This theory sees people as naturally willing to work, able to exercise self-discipline and self-control in certain circumstances, and with the potential for further development. The managerial style favoured here is one of coaxing people through reward, praise, permissiveness and attention.

At the centre of Theory Y is *complex man*. This is a view of the individual which embodies aspects of rational-economic, social and self-actualizing man. Complex man is variable. He has many motives, which form at any one time a hierarchy, although the hierarchy may change from time to time and situation to situation. He can respond to a variety of managerial strategies. Whether he will or not will depend upon his view of their appropriateness to the situation and to his needs.

Viewed in this way, complex man can, given the appropriate conditions at work, show high levels of responsibility and self-direction. The role of management, then, is to create the conditions in which this reservoir of hitherto untapped human resources can be utilized. Given the right conditions, people will be able to achieve their goals best by directing their own efforts towards organizational objectives.

Intuitively, this makes a lot of sense. It also makes possible a plan of action which you as a manager can use.

Satisfaction Theories and Motivation

The ideas of Herzberg and others would seem to suggest that your
aims should be to create satisfying conditions for your employees
and to remove those which cause dissatisfaction. This seems reasonable, but can you be certain that a satisfied employee is necessarily
a productive one?

Research has failed to show a consistent correlation between
employee satisfaction and performance. In fact, common sense
suggests that laid-back, self-satisfied employees may be content to
do no more than the minimum amount of work required to keep
them employed. On the other hand, dissatisfied employees could be
motivated to do much better in order to improve their lot – as long
as they believe that harder work will get them somewhere.

Increases in job satisfaction, therefore, may reduce staff turnover, absenteeism and grievances, but will not necessarily result in
increases in productivity. Satisfaction and performance are often
related, but their precise effect on each other depends on the
working situation and the people in it. People are best motivated
when they have something to strive for. A measure of dissatisfaction
and a desire for more achievement or power may be the best motivator for some people.

Incentive Theories and Motivation

Incentive theories suggest that individuals will increase their efforts
in order to obtain a desired reward – often money. This approach is
based on a rational-economic view of the individual. Such theories
can undoubtedly work, given a certain set of conditions:

1. The person sees the increased reward to be worth the extra
    effort.
2. The performance can be measured and clearly attributed to the
    individual.
3. The individual wants that particular kind of reward.
4. The increased performance will not become the new *minimum*
    standard.

These theories often work well from the owner-manager's point
of view or for employees working in unit or small-batch manufacturing. If, however, any of the first three conditions do not apply, the
individual will tend to see the reward as an improvement to the

general climate of work and will react accordingly (i.e. the reward becomes a hygiene factor, leading to satisfaction but not greater productivity). Violation of condition 4 will do nasty things to a manager's credibility.

Motivation and Performance

The link between motivation and performance would seem to be an obvious one. If individuals are highly motivated, they will perform better. In turn, better performance may well lead to a sense of achievement and result in greater motivation. Thus the relationship between motivation and performance can be a mutually reinforcing one. This, however, begs a number of questions to do with perception, ability and stress.

Yes, motivated employees may do more work, but this may need to be carefully managed if they aren't going to expend most of their energy on aspects of work they find stimulating, which may be of little or no benefit to the company.

Yes, motivated employees may be more productive, providing they have the requisite skills to do the job and the *perception* to realize whether they have or not. It is just as important to take steps to improve *ability* by means of good selection and training as it is to pay attention to motivation.

Lastly, motivation implies pressure – to move forward, to do more – but too much pressure, in other words too much *stress,* can be harmful in both the short and the long term. Short-term signs and symptoms include tiredness, headaches, irritability, sleeplessness, anxiety and frustration. Longer term, there may be a greater likelihood of stomach ulcers, high blood pressure, migraine, asthma, skin conditions, heart disease and strokes – not a very satisfying checklist. Of course, the answer is balance. In the short term, we need sufficient pressure to concentrate well and do the job quickly and efficiently, but not so much that panic starts to intrude and concentration becomes difficult. In the medium to long term, we must avoid working to exhaustion. In terms of Nixon's *human function curve,* this means being just on or to the left of the peak, not beyond the peak to the right (see Figure 2).

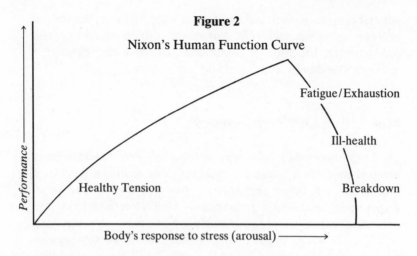

Figure 2

Nixon's Human Function Curve

Putting It All Together – the Complex Model

Where are we going in all this? *Incentive theories* tell us that carrot-and-stick methods are likely to work well with at least some of the people some of the time. People work for rewards. They will work hard if you pay them well and will work harder if you pay them more. If they do not work well, then you sanction them in some way. However, this rational-economic approach is not going to create much commitment above 'a fair day's work for a day's pay'.

Satisfaction theories suggest which factors – Herzberg's hygiene factors – are likely to contribute to a more or less satisfied workforce. But that doesn't necessarily make for a very productive workforce.

And, lastly, the *intrinsic theories* tell us much more about the needs of our employees and how these can be met, to a greater or lesser extent, by an aware and responsive management. Given the right corporate climate, individuals can get at least some of their higher needs met by pursuing company goals.

All of these theories are relevant at one time or another. But how can we make sense of them and put them together in a workable model? Yes, you guessed it. We view the individual as complex and we come up with a model which is a complex model – it draws upon facets of all or most of the theories mentioned so far. How we apply this model will depend on a number of factors, not least our understanding of what motivates *us* in our own lives and how this colours our view of the world, our understanding of what motivates the employee we are dealing with, and the context of that person's job within the organization.

To start with, this complex model can be viewed as the way a person deals with individual/specific/personal decisions (to do or not to do something, to go or not to go, to apportion or not to apportion time, energy and talent). The model presupposes we are (to a greater or lesser extent) self-activating, can control our own destiny and response to outside pressure, and can select goals and choose paths towards them.

We can view the process of motivation as being started when we recognize, consciously or unconsciously, an unsatisfied need. A goal is then established – again, consciously or unconsciously – which we believe will satisfy or help satisfy that need. A course of action is worked out that will lead towards attainment of that goal and, therefore, the satisfaction of the need. Whether we expend time and energy in reaching that goal and satisfying that need will clearly depend on our degree of motivation.

The *strength* of our motivation is going to be dependent on the strength of our need and the *value* of the potential reward, our *experience* as to the success or otherwise of getting this need met, and our *expectation* that a given amount of effort will result in the outcome we want (Figure 3).

Figure 3

The Complex Model of Motivation

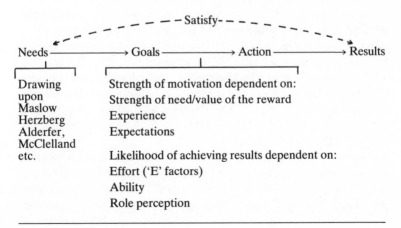

Needs ⟶	Goals ⟶	Action ⟶	Results

Drawing upon Maslow Herzberg Alderfer, McClelland etc.

Strength of motivation dependent on:
Strength of need/value of the reward
Experience
Expectations

Likelihood of achieving results dependent on:
Effort ('E' factors)
Ability
Role perception

The strength of our need will depend on the satisfaction we get *if* we achieve our goal and get our need met. For example, *experience* tells us that some actions bring rewards while others result in failure or even punishment. The rewards act as positive incentives and reinforce the successful behaviour, which is likely to be repeated the next time a similar need emerges. The more powerful, obvious and frequent the reinforcement, the more likely it is to be repeated. On the other hand, failures or punishments suggest that it is necessary to seek alternative means of achieving goals.

The degree to which experience shapes future behaviour depends on the extent to which we recognize the similarity between earlier situations and the one now confronting us. This ability – to perceive and make correlations between one event and other – varies from one person to another. For these reasons, some people are better at learning from experience than others, just as some people are more easily motivated than others.

The existence of this pressure from the past is, of course, an explanation of why people sometimes resist change. If something has worked well in the past, why change it for something that might not work well in the future? (Even if things have not been so good, we may fear that a change will make them worse, since we often have a tendency to expect the worst.)

People will only act if they have a reasonable belief – an *expectation* – that their actions will lead to desired goals. Even if their goals are valued, they will not necessarily aim for them if they think they don't stand a hope in hell of getting there.

Although the strength of expectations may indeed be based on past experiences (reinforcement), individuals are frequently presented with new situations – a change in job, payment system or working conditions imposed by management – where past experience is an inadequate guide to the implications of the change.

Motivation is likely when a clearly perceived and usable relationship exists between the performance and outcome, and the outcome is seen as satisfying needs. This explains why an incentive scheme only works if the link between effort and reward is clear and the value of the reward is worth the effort.

Our model begins to help explain why conscious objective-setting, together with feedback from others as to the results we are achieving, is likely to improve performance in the long run. If we give an individual opportunity to do his or her own motivation 'calculation' based on the strength of the need (the reward for reaching a target), experience and expectations, then that individual is much more likely to reach that target, or give a clear response as to why he/she can't and won't.

Even given high motivation, what determines how likely an individual is to achieve success in their own and in their manager's eyes? Obviously, the amount of *effort*. Charles Handy has come up with a list of what he calls 'E' factors: words that begin with 'E' and characterize the type of effort or energy put in – excitement, enthusiasm, emotion, expenditure (of time, money, passion).

Of course, 'E' on its own isn't enough. It has to be effective 'E' if it is to produce the desired performance. Effectiveness will depend on *ability* and *perception of role* within the organization. The individual needs to have the *ability* – the intelligence, imagination, manual skills, know-how and so on – to carry the strategy through. But individuals also need to have a *perception of the job* being worthwhile in itself and of value to the organization.

The complex model (Figure 3, on page 13) shows us what factors to consider when dealing with people and their motivation. But, and we all know this, life just isn't that simple. The model is useful when you find a motivation problem among a member of staff and you want to get to the bottom of it. It helps ensure you have all the pieces. But what is an effective working philosophy to carry you through from day to day?

Putting It All Together – You as the Manager

Turning people on starts with you. Every interaction you have with your employees may have an influence on their motivation. It will make them more or less likely to 'pull out the stops' when it matters, stay behind after work to finish a project, or to err in your favour in the numerous motivation calculations they make each day.

Be human. We all make mistakes, but at least admit them, and go back and smooth the troubled waters where they occur.

Next, know yourself. Be clear about what motivates you. What are the competing drives – at home and at work – that turn you on? How does this colour the way you see the world, and the way you interact with other people? Typically, the higher up the management hierarchy you are, the more likely you are to identify with the company itself as an institution and have concern for its development. In middle and junior management you are more likely to be concerned with identifying with the success of specific projects for which you have responsibility and control.

At the beginning of this chapter we caught a glimpse of Dave, working outdoors in the cold, and Julia, keen to escape from a meeting. What motivates them? Don't just make broad assumptions about people – ask them, notice their answers and actions, and learn. As managers, while at work, our loyalties are often directed upwards in the management hierarchy. Don't assume loyalties among employees are going to be the same. It is more than likely that their balance of attention at work is directed to their colleagues, and their family and friends.

Turning your team on starts with you. The loyalty and commitment of the team is a function of the commitment you have for it and the determination you have to find out what motivates it.

Chapter 3
The Barriers to Motivation

Britain is a peculiar paradox! Despite the protestations of the Left, it has achieved the not inconsiderable challenge of providing reasonably paid employment for most of its employable population. Wages are higher, *pro rata,* than they have ever been. Hours are shorter, holidays longer. Retirement comes earlier to many. Sick pay comes with the job. Many companies provide welfare and medical advice. There are flexible working arrangements – flexible, that is, for the employees rather than the customers. We have legislated in favour of workers as many – if not more – rights than almost any country in the world.

Yet, we still have a motivation problem – and that's the paradox! We still spend billions of pounds on sick pay, mainly to people who aren't sick. We spend billions more subsidizing (I'm not saying it's wrong) the right of people to strike for better conditions of employment. We have one of the worst export and manufacturing records in Europe (where we *do* manage to provide goods for foreign markets in the right quantity and at the right price, we find that we're majoring in television sets, while the Germans are doing it with motor cars and machine tools).

And it's never our fault. We've always got hundreds of excuses (any permutation will do):

> Inflationary pay demands by trade unions; lazy workers; Japanese import controls; the Bundesbank; cost of imported materials; failure of government to reduce or abolish taxes; VAT; climate; greenhouse effect; lack of understanding by workers of facts of economic life . . .

We have problems and excuses in spades. Maybe all the problems are genuine and real – perhaps every excuse holds water. But the solutions are simple and straightforward. They are to be found in two simple words – management and motivation.

Management and Motivation

So why is motivation so difficult? Why is it that we have so many
problems persuading people who work in this once great economy
to do simple things like turn up to work on time every day, produce
good-quality goods and services in the right volumes and amounts?
What are the factors that so inevitably turn people off? Here are
some 'general' ones:

A. Size

A few years ago I was present at a conference in London. One
of the first speakers was a major industrialist who was asked
the question: 'Why is your company involved in so many
acquisitions?' His reply was simple: 'Because, in 20 years or
so, I think that the British economy will be dominated by
around 100-200 organizations, and I intend that mine shall be
one of them.'

Most of us wouldn't wish to argue with the logic of that statement. We live in the age of Hanson and Goldsmith, Maxwell and
Murdoch. And it's undeniably true. Organizations *are* getting bigger
all the time, and it's very difficult to feel wanted and significant when
you're just one employee working in a great big conglomerate.
Maybe it's not impossible – but it's certainly very, very difficult. It's
all very well for chief executives to talk about teamwork. But most
successful teams have eleven or fifteen players. Not 28,000.

So size is a problem if you believe, as I do, that part of the key to
motivation is that people should feel important, as individuals,
know where they fit into the scheme of things, and be able to make
their contribution felt.

A major manufacturing company changed its structure and
introduced the concept of manufacturing 'centres'. In each
discrete 'centre', dedicated to a simple product or set of
products, process operators, engineers and quality-assurance
specialists all work alongside each other on a double day and
night shift. At the bottom, the section managers control
'teams' of up to 30 or 40 people. Gradually the company is
breaking these 'teams' down into groups of 10-15 individuals,
under technicians or foremen. The reason? Simple enough –
they keep finding that one person can't control and motivate
30 or 40 at the same time.

A few years ago, a friend of mine was carrying out a management and supervisory training assignment in a motor manufacturer. While he was 'walking the job', he talked to a

supervisor. The company was very concerned about the role of supervisors, and particularly anxious that their self-esteem should be protected. (There was a great deal of trade union activity, which inevitably meant that shop stewards were better informed than supervisors.) So supervisors were given a uniform (better not described here, but easily imagined or remembered!) That was how my colleague recognized the person to whom he was talking. 'So what do you do here?'

'Well, I'm a line supervisor.'

'What does that mean?'

'I run this section of the line.'

'How many people is that?'

'About 75.'

'75 people! How on earth do you do it?'

'How do I do *what?*'

'How do you communicate with them? How do you consult them? How do you set targets? How do you give them a pat on the back or a prod? How do you keep them going? How do you manage discipline? How do you manage to ensure that they listen to you as well as the shop steward?'

'Well, with 75 people – how would *you* do it?'

'I don't think I could.'

'Well, since you put it like that, I don't think I do.'

Another problem with size is the remoteness people feel when the decisions that affect them are taken a long way away.

In a food-manufacturing company, it was decided some years ago to introduce a major cost-cutting initiative, combined with a big investment programme and profound changes in working practices and corporate culture. It was a very ambitious project and has undoubtedly been enormously successful, when measured in terms of profitability. What is undeniably also true is that while senior executives saw the programme as composed of a number of equally important initiatives, employees at the bottom of the heap saw it as a cost-cutting and numbers exercise. 'Call it a "culture change" if you want,' said a shop steward. 'But down here it's spelt R-E-D-U-N-D-A-N-C-Y!' It's taken this particular organization over five years to persuade employees of its sincerity of purpose.

Without any doubt at all, size is a major barrier to overcome. While nobody can prevent organizations from becoming bigger, it has to be understood that however big the company or corporation becomes, structure has to be managed so as to preserve the dignity and esteem of individuals. And if you don't? They might bring their bodies to work, but they'll leave their hearts and minds behind.

B. Job design

If you and I had to do some of the jobs we ask other people to do, we'd die of boredom or go mad. Can you imagine sitting in a supermarket, passing bar codes over an electronic eye so that a computer can add up the customer's account, adjust the stock take and print out the sales ticket, all in one easy hi-tech movement?

> The Industrial Society tells the story of a customer in a major supermarket in Europe. He queued at the till patiently until finally it was his turn. He unloaded his trolley and, in complete silence, his transaction was completed as the assistant removed each article, passed the bar code over the electronic eye, and deposited it on another pile next to the plastic bags provided. At the end of this stage of the transaction, the assistant solemnly passed him the sales ticket, and the following conversation ensued.
> Customer: 'Marvellous thing, technology, isn't it?'
> Assistant: 'Sorry?'
> Customer: 'Marvellous, these computers, aren't they?'
> Assistant: 'What do you mean?'
> Customer: 'Well, just look at what's been happening here. A few years ago you'd have had to look at the price of each article and ring it up. We might have had to talk to each other. In fact, you might even have ended up saying "Thank you".'
> Assistant: 'I don't have to do that any more. It's already printed on the ticket.'

Such is progress, we may say. And yet the impact of 'progress' upon motivation is profound indeed. At a far more sophisticated level, ask any printer about the impact of computerized technology on typesetting. It was only yesterday that typesetting was a matter of skill and judgement and considerable hand-eye co-ordination . Nowadays, all you need is some reasonably sophisticated software and a course in computer awareness.

Yet what is work without pride? Is not work an expression of self-esteem? Shouldn't people feel proud of what they do?

> In a component manufacturers, I found myself talking to a lady who had no idea at all of the significance of the component which she was assembling. When I later found out and told her that it was the part of a telephone that actually enabled the caller to talk to someone in another country, she was thrilled and upset. 'Why didn't anyone tell me before?'

I read somewhere recently that more has been invented in the past 50 years than in the whole of the earlier history of mankind. In fact, it's not difficult to see that as technology progresses, and demand for it accelerates, all work will be de-humanized. Already we have driverless trains. Already people are talking about aeroplanes that won't need pilots. Manufacturing and robotics are becoming synonymous.

Those humans that do remain will undoubtedly have removed from their duties any activities which are prone to human error. We're going to be confronted by employees who have very little to do. And, if we're not very careful, that minimal demand will quickly translate itself into resentment and frustration. We will have to look again at issues like job design. Yet experience shows that financial arguments for automation need to take account of other factors.

> On a new rapid-transit system, the Docklands Light Railway, one of the key employees is 'the Train Captain'. DLR has trains that don't need drivers and stations that don't need staff. You can buy your ticket from a machine and get off at your destination, unchecked. The Train Captain is in charge of your train. He or she checks your ticket, collects money and can control both the train and doors. DLR has, quite correctly, worked out that its customers don't like fully automated trains, which eliminate the human element altogether. So they've employed Train Captains for their ability to relate to customers. The customer has become the focal point of the service. The Train Captain is DLR's means of demonstrating this.

C. Money

There's not much to say about money, except that Herzberg was right. Dead on the nail. Have you ever met anyone who talked about his or her salary except to complain – either that it wasn't enough, or wasn't as much as the next guy, or was unfairly worked out? So let's quickly repeat the litany:

1. We all need it
2. There's never enough of it
3. It always de-motivates.
4. It matters like hell – but there is more to work than money.

That's about the long and short of it. If you don't agree, then nothing I can think of to say is going to change your mind. There is, however, an important distinction to be made between 'reward' and 'recognition' and we shall return to this in Chapter 9.

D. Pre-conditioning

'Give me the child and I will give you the man' is an aphorism much
suited to management.

> During the 1970s, when I was working for the Industrial
> Society, I once went to chair what was called a 'Challenge of
> Industry' conference. Such events are run in schools to give
> older pupils some idea about the world of work. There's a talk
> from a manager, and another from a trade union representative,
> and much of the programme is spent in groups, discussing
> and solving employee-relations problems. I've always
> thought them to be very useful.
>
> This particular conference was held at one school while
> boys and girls from other local comprehensives were bussed
> in. In the evening we were being transported back to some
> school or other, when the bus passed through an industrial
> estate at the top of which was a famous perfume factory, a
> household name.
>
> 'There you are, girls,' said Miss whoever she was, 'That's
> where you go if you fail your "O" levels.'

Since then, I have frequently taken part in discussions or meetings at schools or universities, and invariably been introduced as
though I were a Martian or some kind of roué who had been unlucky
or undeserving and had thus not been able to qualify for one of the
small number of occupations that some educationalists regard as
being the only acceptable ones.

It might be wise, therefore, not to rely too much on the educational system to equip recruits with a decent idea of what work is
really like. For example, some schools are still highly autocratic
places in which rules and regulations are regarded as paramount.
Pupils from such schools are likely to find it difficult to cope with
some of the freedoms and responsibilities that work can offer. They
can present a motivational problem all of their own, maybe frightened to take decisions, unwilling to take responsibility.

Yet other schools are free-for-alls, in which discipline is lax and
attendance and standards difficult to enforce. School leavers from
such places find it difficult to adjust to the uniformity of the work place.

Some schools (and certainly most places of further education) are
very democratic places, in which 'having a say' is regarded as
commonplace and it is assumed that you will in some way be
involved in decision-making. Again, this can sometimes present
real problems at work.

People who have been to work already will invariably have been
conditioned by their experience to expect or suspect an environment
which is different from what they actually get. Yet how many

organizations have induction programmes or training schemes which accommodate the need to help people *adjust their values, beliefs and expectations* over a period of time?

E. Machismo

Consider how some managers actually behave. Here is a list of true quotations gathered over the years and to be found in any Rambo-esque managers' vocabulary:

'Why can't they just do what they're bloody well told?'
'I haven't got *time* to consult. What do you think this place is, Moscow?'
'They get paid for it, don't they?'
'The unwashed? All they care about is money.'
'People hate change . . . Can't see the wood for the trees?'
'My people don't need objectives. They know their jobs?'
'If they have a problem, they can ask?'
'I haven't got time to hold meetings. I've got a business to run.'
'Why don't they come into the real world?'
'If you talk to them, they argue.'

I still run training sessions on motivation at which such expressions are commonplace. Yet what is ironic is the way in which the people who coin them are always talking about someone else – never themselves.

It may be a man's world out there – but it could do with a few less 'manly' values. Machismo or Rambo-style management is, in my experience, an enormous barrier to commitment and motivation. We have somehow bred a generation of managers whose instincts and inclinations are not in the least complementary to the world in which they have to manage.

Never has this world been more competitive. Staying alive, continual improvement, total quality, cost effectiveness – all are crucial elements in today's business world. They all mean *change,* planning it, pacing it, costing it, monitoring it – and, above all, if you employ people, helping them to live with it. One of the effects of the 'demographic time bomb' is that, very soon, Britain will simply run out of raw recruits. *Retraining and retention* are going to become major elements in any management kit-bag of skills. *Yet both require a fundamental interest and belief in people as a necessary asset.* Managers who are unable to motivate employees to live with and believe in change will simply lose their staff. Any 'style', if style it can be called, of management which implies that it is namby-pamby to care for employees will militate against the working environment upon which change depends. There are some managers about who shouldn't have their names on their office doors. They'd be better off with a sign which said: 'Beware of the Rottweiler.' A few of them would even be pleased about it.

D. Trade unions

It isn't the trade union's job to manage people at work. The system doesn't work like that. It simply isn't true that all management has to do is come to some sort of agreement with the trade union representatives and then expect them to sell the need for change to their constituents (the company's employees). And yet, here we are, in the 1990s and still we're confronted by management/union disputes in which employers complain that 'The union is not controlling its members.'

Unions *don't* control members any more, if they ever did. The reality is that members control unions (see Figure 4). Managements that want good union relationships (and most of them would claim to do so) should bear in mind that the only way to achieve such an objective *in the long term* is by making the members happy, not the shop stewards. It is not part of a shop steward's job to be happy – or, indeed, to preach happiness and the need to be content with your

Figure 4

Trade Unions and Motivation

The line of authority *doesn't* work like this:

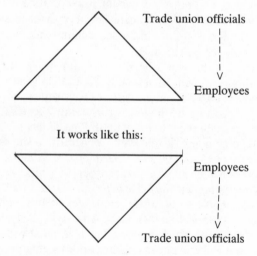

It's called democracy – and, in the final analysis, it works.

lot. Shop stewards who advise people to knuckle down and accept managements offer (final or not) of 4 per cent tend not to be re-elected.

Trade unions, whether or not employers *agree,* see their role as being one of improving the conditions of their subscribers. They don't, on the whole, see why they should co-operate with schemes which set out to cut jobs, or make working life in some way more inconvenient. It's a mystery why managers don't cotton onto this and concentrate their efforts on managing communications well, instead of simply trying to seduce trade union representatives who've seen much of it before!

> An airline decided to eliminate a few less important routes from its schedule. The passenger uptake had been low and losing them would cause little upheaval. It approached its trade unions' chairman and secured agreement that such a change wouldn't be seriously challenged.
>
> A few months later, the airline went back to the unions and said that another set of routes had become unprofitable and that it was taking steps to eliminate these as well. This time the unions riposted. The airline argued a precedent had been set. The unions said they wouldn't agree until they'd seen the accounts. The accounts – maybe with some reluctance – were duly handed over and the unions asked whether they might be allowed the opportunity of suggesting alternatives. The management said there were no alternatives. But the unions persisted and were finally given a week's 'stay of execution'.
>
> One week later, the unions presented a business plan for running the routes and making them profitable. It involved aircrew selling tickets and loading bags and various other changes in working practices. The airline accepted the plans – although not without scepticism and no little annoyance that the unions had changed the rules (after all, nobody had told *them* that pilots would agree to load bags!). The routes are still being run in the same way and this part of the airline is profitable.

The moral of this story, however, is not that unions are always right and employers are always wrong; it's that change is a function of *consent.* Management cannot demand and secure consent as some kind of right. And trade unions cannot grant consent on behalf of their members. They are not so empowered. Before guaranteeing that pilots would load bags, they had to ask them. And if you're wondering why management didn't think of that, then you're not alone!

It isn't the trade union's job to 'turn on' their members (your employees). Relying on them to do this job as well as their own often has the opposite effect.

There are a number of factors at work which all conspire to undermine commitment and motivation. This chapter has examined a few of them. Frequently personnel specialists are blamed for badly motivated workforces. *But motivation isn't their job. It's a manager's job.* After all, line management wants the credit for results – and quite rightly.

The personnel specialist's role is advisory; the rest of this book looks at the practical advice managers need in order to provide for motivation, enthusiasm or, if you prefer, a sense of urgency. They are the difference between turning people *on* and turning them off.

Always keep in mind the direct initial impact on workpeople of changes in personnel policy. Consider, for example, the effect of a 30 per cent pay rise over three years. The intention, of course, is to secure recruitment policy and stem the drift of employees away to better paid jobs elsewhere. As demographic shifts and trends make themselves felt, we will inevitably see more and more of this.

Much more important, however, is the effect of such an initiative on motivation. What does the average employee say when suddenly told that her wages are to be increased by 15 per cent overnight without being aware of having done anything to justify it? Does she say: 'Gosh! How generous! Now I must work even harder'? Or does she say: 'They must be crazy! Still, I'll take the money'? Your guess is as good as mine.

Chapter 4
The Influence of Personnel

Personnel managers are clearly in a unique position to influence the success of their organizations. However, unless personnel policy is *initiatory* in its nature, it is all too easy for their role to revert to one of solving problems.

Obviously, there has to be more to life than this, and in this chapter I have tried to set out a simple model which, in my experience, can help personnel managers take initiatives for ensuring that the organization and its people are managed in a mutually complementary way (see Figure 5, page 28).

The model shows all the key elements, but unless each element's management needs are treated as, if not complementary, then at least not in conflict with the others, the personnel manager's role will invariably be seen as simply administrative. Yet the theme that runs through any organization is *people* and the key to success in any business is to achieve the right linkages between *people* and *results*. Personnel management is therefore as much about influencing the way people are *managed* as it is about how they are recruited, trained and paid.

The Core Values of the Business

All organizations are driven by a series of 'core values'. Generically expressed, these values are about:

> Quality
> Output
> Time
> Cost
> Customers/Consumers
> Safety.

Most smart companies or organizations quickly realize that success depends on your ability to control not just a couple of these

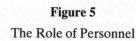

Figure 5

The Role of Personnel

core values – but all of them at the same time. If, for example, you concentrate too much on achieving output or volume targets, then unit costs will explode as you spend too much money on overtime or on wages for temporary labour. If you put all your energy into controlling costs, then frequently both output and quality are put at risk as managers skimp on raw materials or inspection techniques. If you do everything your customers ask for, you'll go out of business in no time at all.

Now consider the effect of *people* on all of those core values and measures. It's pretty obvious that, in every case, the human factor is absolutely crucial. It shouldn't need a genius to understand that badly motivated, badly directed employees can and will undermine every performance target, and that *effective* management is therefore about achieving results through *people*. Yet how many managers actually have – and set for other managers – objectives which relate to the management of people?

So the first step in making the influence of the personnel specialist felt lies in helping to define the accountability of line managers for managing, *through people,* those core values of the business.

There is a clear link between the issues upon which any business depends for its success, its managers and its employees. All three elements contribute to – and can undermine – each other. Yet many managers have difficulty in effecting the linkages. They don't see the problem like that. Sometimes they haven't defined the core values anyhow, and sometimes they are tempted to see employees as obstacles to the achievement of success, rather than as facilitators.

An important *first* step, therefore, for any personnel specialist is to influence line management accountability.

- Help managers define the key values

- Demonstrate the way key values depend on people

- Define accountabilities.

Recruitment, Selection and Induction of non-management employees

You can ensure that recruitment and selection standards take into account social skills and abilities as well as technical standards.

> When an overseas manufacturer started up in Great Britain on a greenfield site, employing local labour, everyone who applied for employment was given, to start with, a test covering numeracy, literacy and manual dexterity. That was before any interviewing took place. Subsequently, interviews and a series of semi-social events were arranged to ensure that recruits at management level not only understood but could practice good communication skills.

It seems obvious to me that it is no longer possible to appoint people to positions – and particularly to managerial positions – simply because they meet the technical requirements. Because the links between people and quality and between quality and competitiveness are undeniable, it's more important than ever before to ensure that selection takes account of human skills and characteristics *as well as* technical standards or educational qualifications. After all, employees like their colleagues to be not only competent but also acceptable.

Another key issue today is flexibility. Unless you consciously decide to be flexible about whom you recruit, you'll simply end up fishing in a smaller and smaller pool. This, in turn, affects motivation.

Induction

The most important and influential period of employment is the first year. After that, it may be too late. So ensure that induction programmes accommodate the values and standards you believe matter. Ensure induction programmes are practical and well presented. Ensure that they discuss the *way* you work, and not just the package of pay and conditions that accompanies the job.

> One major public utility has recently introduced a new induction programme which majors on three key factors: Efficiency; Safety; Customer Care. The programme contains a balance of booklets, a managers' manual and a video and concentrates on helping new entrants to recognize what has to be done at their level to help the enterprise run efficiently, safely and with the maximum regard for its customers. The last part of the programme describes the package of pay and conditions which you the employee receive, *provided you honour your part of the bargain.*

Managing Performance

You can ensure that your organization adopts and supports a sound performance management policy. This should mean that, at every level, the results required are defined in advance and that the management climate is consciously adapted to support the achievement of results. In practical terms, this means:

- Clear job descriptions at every level, stating
  - the purpose of the job
  - the main areas of responsibility
  - *standards of performance*
  - simple priorities which must be achieved in order to protect standards.
- Structure and teamwork
  - Employees should be organized into teams under clearly defined and accountable leaders. (Where there are common working interests, these should be accommodated in the same team; don't have operators working for one boss and, say, maintenance fitters working for another.)
  Keep the size of teams to a sensible minimum. Fifteen is about the optimum size. A team of 80 people is *not* a team.

- Regular performance review
  - It is no use relying on an annual performance appraisal exercise. Nobody's performance can be effectively managed by reviewing it *only* once a year. Each employee ought to have an informal review with his or her supervisor every few weeks, when requirements and standards, progress and achievement are the main items on the agenda.

- Training/Instruction
  - Employees at every level need regular coaching and support. Since it is clearly impractical to organize this on a central basis, you should ensure that managers are themselves well trained and equipped with basic skills in coaching, so that they can contribute to meeting training needs.

- Non-Achievers
  - There should be a policy for trying to support non-achievers, but, if necessary, remove them. It's painful and not always easy to face. But it's also a fact of life that some people simply can't cope. Remember to use the discipline procedure constructively – but don't avoid its use. Non-achievers are what it's for.

- High Achievers
  - There needs to be a policy (see page 76).

Performance-Related Pay

Much is written and said about performance-related pay, as if this were some kind of panacea. However, the fact is that you already *do* pay for performance in your wages and salary policy. Therefore, any innovation called performance-related pay can, by definition, *only reward certain aspects of performance.*

Until you have established a sound performance-management system, you shouldn't introduce performance-related pay.

Here are some common sense tips:

- Pay for the whole job
- Reward only when standard is exceeded (or at least met)
- Don't fudge the standards so that everyone gets an extra rise without achieving anything extra. (In other words, don't pay extra for what people *ought to be doing anyhow.*)
- Don't allow pay to undermine performance management. (For example, if someone *is* a non-achiever, and you're seriously considering discipline, don't let some idiot give them a merit increase.)
- Make the reward significant enough to bother about.

Bear in mind that once you introduce bad habits, sloppy standards and anomalies into your pay policy, it's really difficult to eliminate them. So unless you genuinely believe in and can support merit-ocratic principles, don't introduce them until your organization is ready.

The Management Appraisal System

Personnel managers have the opportunity to influence formal appraisal systems as well as informal performance review. However, in too many organizations, appraisal systems have become white elephants. The reason is simple. Over-complication! It is difficult to understand why any normal person would want to fill in a complicated form about someone else, especially a form which is couched in jargon which is difficult to understand. Yet on the introduction of many appraisal systems this is precisely what many line managers are asked to do. Why not instead influence policy at the top and go for something much more simple?

1. A requirement that management performance *must* be reported on objectively.
2. A requirement that performance must take account of 'people' as well as technical and numerate issues.
3. A requirement that training and development potential must be covered in the report.
4. A requirement to express in ordinary language what is required (Ask seriously if a manager not literate enough to do this really deserves his or her job!)
5. A requirement that each manager must see his or her boss *at least* every month in order to discuss performance against objectives.

Management Development

We've already suggested that the problem for some managers is *making the right links between people and results*. The fact that some people find this difficult isn't surprising.

> Talking recently to the young general manager of a factory, I was interested to hear him say that if he'd known five years ago what he knew how, he'd have approached the challenge of management at senior level quite differently. When I asked why, he summed it up like this: 'When I was running a depart-ment I would carry a small group of managers — and all I had

was a small group – with my own enthusiasm. When they
didn't do what I wanted, I had time to stop and coach them.
But now I'm running a factory, I can't enthuse them all.
There's plenty of room in the system to hide – and I've had to
learn the hard way that you can't assume that other people
will ever do naturally what you do naturally yourself.'

On the bottom line, managers are promoted for many reasons
other than some innate ability to lead, motivate and inspire others.
Sometimes it's a matter of seniority, sometimes it's a question of
technical proficiency (and has to be). But it's wrong to assume that
qualities which aren't naturally present in a manager's make-up, at
the time of the appointment, will somehow manifest themselves as
time goes on. It just doesn't work like that!

One way in which our competitors take advantage of us is in their
standards of management training. The Japanese, in particular, are
very conscious of the need to influence management behaviour to
help link people and results.

'But you can't make bricks without straw,' say the protesters – to
which the answer is 'Sometimes you can.' Many management development and training experts have discovered through extensive
research that you can take very ordinary, uncharismatic managers
and teach them to put into practice what successful managers do.
'By doing they become' is the experience.

Checklist

Managers won't all *naturally* do the following things, but they can be
shown how to:

- structure their teams into manageable units
- set targets, write job descriptions
- consult upon/discuss improvements
- communicate progress
- manage discipline
- monitor standards
- manage employee representatives
- manage the fair implementation of procedures
- review performance
- ensure that terms and conditions of employment are fairly applied
- train and coach their teams.

Personnel managers should ask themselves how competent they believe their line managers to be in these areas. If they're honest, they'll admit that, for many, these techniques (and that's all they are) are something of a mystery. If they're not *shown* how to do these things, they won't often learn them as they go along. Instead, they'll acquire bad habits, together with a fierce and false sense of pride which makes them very unwilling to abandon them.

Communication and Consultation

More is written about these issues than almost any other aspect of human resource management. So muted is the effect that you could be forgiven for wondering whether anyone out there is listening at all! What is abundantly clear is that, for many line managers, employee communications are still either a mystery or far too difficult to manage. Britain is not unique in its difficulties, but it has a problem, just like other industrial nations. What *does* make Britain unique is the fact that far too many enterprises have no communication standards at all. Here are a few to be going on with:

1. Every organization should have an employee-communication strategy, linked to its business objectives and setting out *what* needs to be communicated and *by whom.*
2. There should be a simple statement which expresses the organization's commitment (see the example in Chapter 10, page 83).
3. There should be an annual plan which summarizes *what* will be communicated, *when,* and *who* will be accountable for it.
4. Management should be held accountable through clearly expressed management objectives.
5. Trade union representatives should be accountable *only* for communicating union business.
6. Communication should be *regular, face-to-face* and, at the workplace, in *teams.*
7. Provision should be made for senior management visibility.
8. Communication should be regularly monitored against clearly understood and accepted benchmarks.
9. There should be clearly defined methods for communicating *upward* as well as *downward.*
10. Training should be regularly provided in communication skills.

For too many personnel managers, employee communications are a very limited affair: explaining to just a few management's position with regard to why/how the business is developing; an employee report here and there, and some concentration on joint consultative machinery. This is as much as they can achieve on their own; the rest is down to line management. Yet since many line managers don't see communication as being part of their job, this is another opportunity to exert influence.

Terms and Conditions of Employment

Personnel managers have more influence on these issues than anyone else. On their own, pay and conditions make personnel managers more important, give them more power, than any other single factor. Almost on their own, personnel managers have introduced:

> Contracts, Service agreements, Grievance procedures, Discipline procedures, Disputes procedures, Redundancy procedures, Job-evaluation procedures, Appeal procedures, Piecework, Daywork, Payment by results, Holiday pay, Sick pay, Works rules, Pension policies, Early retirement, Equal pay, Equal opportunity, Ethnic group policies, AIDS and employment policies, Drug abuse policies, Alcohol policies, Welfare policies, Health and safety policies, Hygiene policies, Car parking and canteen policies, etc.

There is one factor that all these policies and initiatives have in common. Wherever they are managed *positively*, nobody abuses them. The more complicated they are, the more devious the 'beneficiaries' (your employees) will become. Everybody knows examples of bonus schemes that don't provide any incentive, prosperity schemes which might help employees but do little for organizational prosperity. Of course, a certain amount of bureaucracy is inevitable in a society which imposes so much legislation upon its citizens. But for all that there is a clear onus of responsibility upon employers (and hence personnel managers) to

- Simplify procedures
- Explain them
- Show how/why they matter

- and not continually quote them as obstacles to progress.

Finally, attention should be paid as soon as possible to harmonizing terms and conditions of employment, to eliminate unfairness and create an environment in which trust is a watchword (see Chapter 7).

Workplace Industrial Relations

The interface between trade union and employer is frequently the
personnel department. Personnel managers are normally the re-
cipients of claims or requests made by trade unions or their
representatives. Their position uniquely equips them to influence
both the behaviour of trade union towards management, and
management towards trade union. It is important, therefore, that
relationships with trade unions should not be clothed in any more
mystique than is necessary; fundamental standards should be established in order for them to be generally regarded in a productive
light.

1. Ensure all management/union communications are open and can
   be seen by *everyone* to be open.

   > One organization recently introduced a policy of Total Quality
   > Management and, rightly, took a decision that leadership from
   > the top was a fundamental prerequisite. The Works Council's
   > involvement was therefore sought and obtained, and a series
   > of Works Council meetings arranged to cement the joint
   > commitment to improving quality. Shortly afterwards, an
   > independently conducted communication audit showed that
   > employees thought that the Works Council was a remote
   > elitist group.

2. Establish a jointly agreed procedure for managing communication during the process of negotiation.

   > A distribution company jointly agrees a series of messages
   > about the progress of negotiations:
   > a.   joint statement describing initial claim and response
   > b.   joint statement describing any improvements
   > c.   joint statement describing final settlement.
   >
   > All messages are factual and devoid of emotive or adjectival
   > qualifications such as 'The unions have not yet accepted this
   > very reasonable (and final) offer . . .'

3. Manage communications through the line and not through the
   trade union hierarchy.

   Nothing so undermines management authority than employees
finding out what's happening from an elected representative.

   > A print company uses its 'chapel' (shop stewards) commit-
   > tees as the focal point of all communications. 'Fathers of the

chapel' (shop stewards) are the prime communicators of all information. Consequence: junior managers and supervisors refuse to take any responsibility which involves changing procedures or working practices until senior management has first agreed the changes with FOC's. The company is (literally) going out of business with awesome rapidity.

4. Encourage as many moderates as possible to join trade unions and take part in activities. In this way, sensible influence can frequently be brought to bear on more enthusiastic members!

Chapter 5
A Management Style for the 90s

Almost every measurable aspect of business *depends,* at least to some extent, on the human factor. Yet, as organizations cut their costs in order to become more competitive, or to meet budgetary constraints, they are often obliged to decrease their staff. Depleted labour forces, in turn, can become more and more difficult to motivate, and the role of management becomes ever more important.

Employee profiles are changing too. In the 90s many people will be working in a competitive labour market, one in which their skills and abilities are at a premium. They won't all have to grab – and be grateful for the first job that comes along. Furthermore, they don't simply bring their brains to work. They also bring their feelings, their emotions, and their problems. And many have more problems – at least potentially – than ever before. Most of these are familiar enough. They're the outcome of the twentieth century's economic and social difficulties, and include problems of money, stress, drugs, alcohol and a variety of diet-related issues like cholesterol excess, and high blood pressure. Like it or not, these matters are part of the challenge of contemporary management. They exist, and they'll probably get worse. If we are to come to terms with change, they will have to be managed. Failing to face them will result in a host of other problems – absenteeism, staff turnover, service faults – and so on. Remember, Britain still has an absence rate of around 5 per cent, or about two weeks away from work per year, for every employee.

In addition to all this, there are also more pressures upon employees at work today, which make the motivational challenge an even steeper one. These pressures include: boredom (many new jobs are simply less stimulating than the ones they replaced), unsocial hours, constant pressure to achieve demanding volume/ output targets or quality standards, constant cost cutting and a difficult industrial-relations climate. For many work people the combination of such factors is very difficult to cope with.

All too often, the result is employees who either opt out or become more aggressive. Of course, they don't *all* behave like this. There are many variations on an original theme of frustration and some people are much better adjusted than others. But the difficulty for personnel specialists is to equip their organizations with line managers who are up to handling the potential issues. Smart organizations already do this, but others have either not yet realized the problem – or are handling it in a quite inappropriate way.

How not to handle frustration

DON'T compel all your managers to attend courses on managing stress (or any other concept you haven't defined in organizational terms).

DON'T ignore it and hope that it won't come or that it will go away (it won't).

DON'T look at easy options, such as increasing shift premia or altering bonus structures. Remember that today's 'productivity' increase is tomorrow's abuse!

How to come to terms with it

DO take an objective look at the problem as it applies to your company or organization. Carry out a survey, even if it has to be crude and workmanlike. Consider carefully the reasons for absence, the nature of the work/jobs. Talk to employees about the way they feel, how they cope, why they stay with your organization, what they would seek from alternative sources of employment etc.

DO *plan for a management 'style' that's appropriate to the needs of these changing times.*

We will now look in more detail at what that actually means.

A Management Style for the 90s

Eliminate the Machismo Factor

As I've already said, some managers are a little too keen to indulge their own sense of machismo. Maybe they're dominated at home too much, maybe their fathers or mothers were too hard on them. But, whatever the reason, a style of behaviour that says 'Don't bother me' or 'I suffered, why shouldn't you' is often *not* what your organization needs.

'But we depend on their technical skills,' the protesters cry. 'We don't employ our managers for their kindness and sensitivity. This is a hard cruel world, etc.' Sorry, they're missing the point. And they're wrong! You employ managers to manage and part of that is to manage *people* in a caring way which is complementary to your organization's objectives. If managers don't have these skills, or won't learn them; if *you* won't develop them, or can't teach them, then

you're employing the wrong managers

OR you're using the wrong training methods

OR the organization has the wrong personnel policy

OR you're wrong for the job you do.

Yet the plain facts are that none of your managers (unless they were trained in the Waffen SS or a prison hulk) are *naturally* inhuman brutes. Your managers are fathers and mothers, husbands and wives. They're citizens – normal members of society. They only behave like that at work. Why? Because *you* don't set out what's required, or at least not often enough.

Communication skills

Do your managers know that they're supposed to *talk* to people and *listen* to them? Have you taught – (or had taught) some basic counselling techniques so that they can use and develop their own powers of observation and nip problems in the bud before they become issues? Do they understand what is meant by expressions like 'brief' and 'consult' or 'listen'?

> A management survey carried out in a major public utility in 1990, showed that fewer than 30 per cent of all managers had received any training in basic communication skills and techniques. This organization loses money, has a lamentable safety record and is much vilified and criticized by the media for its scant regard for its customers.

Education

Do your managers receive from/through the organization, regular input and information about the world in which they live and manage? How much do they know about socio-economic conditions in your area or region? How much do they know about drugs, about alcohol and alcoholism?

Other training needs

Have your managers been trained in problem-solving skills (human and otherwise)? Have they received training in team leadership and team working? Do they know how to set objectives, carry out a performance review or manage their time? Do you have an adequate training budget? Is your training manager or training officer up to the requirements of the job? Do you personally influence the selection of outside consultants?

Monitoring/support

Do you personally monitor the effect and impact of management style in your organization? What, incidentally do you think personnel management is about – *this,* or something else? Do you check to see that the organization keeps its promises and pledges? Do you ever blindly, or out of a sense of misplaced loyalty, back managers who make silly, rash or hotheaded decisions? Do you look for good examples of 'people management' and tell other people about them? Do you know the achievers – or the free-loaders – by name? Are you doing anything to ensure that the former are recognized and the latter dealt with?

A fair deal

Are your managers fairly treated? Is there a proper relationship between pay and achievement? When they receive a 'merit' increase, do they know why? Do they know what their projected career pattern is? Do they have regular access to their boss? Do they have clearly defined goals or targets?

Clarity

Have your organization's standards for the management of people been written down and published? Are they written in job descriptions? Do they form part of the performance appraisal process?

> A multiple retailer circulated its 'People Policy' to every employee. It describes in simple terms, on one page, its intention to treat people fairly, communicate regularly, set goals and targets, consult on change, and hold line managers accountable for employees' well-being. This organization is now one of Britain's top 50 employers with an enviable track record of profits.

Decision-taking

Have managers in your organization been taught:

- how to evaluate options
- how to manage consultation
- how to plan the timing of a decision
- how to explain decisions
- how to check that they're working.

Justice

Do your managers know how to administer *justice?* No, not how to sit in judgement on people but how to manage terms and conditions, rules and regulations, in a fair and *just* manner. Unnecessary inconsistencies only delay and divert attention from business priorities. You can't just talk about equality – you have to practice it.

> A food processing company had been moving towards 'harmonization' of terms and conditions of employment for some two years. In order to speed up the process, the Operations Director, Deputy MD and General Manufacturing Manager all voluntarily surrendered *their* offices in favour of open plan.

Accountability

Effective line management demands both being accountable and insisting on accountability. Have your organizational responsibilities for managers been defined at all levels? Does your organization insist on responsibilities being met and observed?

Technical proficiency

Finally, are your managers, particularly middle managers and supervisors, technically proficient enough to demonstrate credibility and provide real leadership instead of mere 'cheer' leadership?

But, surely, you say, all that is terribly obvious. Well yes, it *is* – but does it happen?

You may think it's simply not possible to create such paragons of virtue. You may be asking what you're supposed to do with your existing managers who don't conform to these rather high (and maybe) new standards. Sack them? Transfer them? Train them? Tell them to change their spots?

Nobody said any of this was necessarily easy. And the answer to these questions may be that it's impossible. But a management style which is appropriate for the 90s and beyond, demands that you should seek to change behaviour wherever it *is* possible and fundamentally necessary. And it certainly demands that when you're recruiting or selecting managers and supervisors, you look for the existence of (or at least the potential for developing) a number of basic attributes in addition to numeracy and literacy. These include:

Communication skills
Education in contemporary values including socio-economics
Problem-solving abilities
Ability to listen
Decision-taking ability
A sense of justice and fairness
Understanding the meaning of accountability
Technical proficiency.

How near are your managers to the ideal?

On a scale of 1 to 5 (5 being totally acceptable and 1 being totally unacceptable), award your own line management colleagues a score. Probably, most of them will score at least 3 or 4. So the amount by which their behaviour has to be changed isn't immense, although there will be a few individuals who simply won't do and whose responsibilities you may have to alter. But is that really so difficult? Why is it you can contemplate painting round or over the crack, when what it really needs is mending?

Take another look at your training and education policies. Examine the scope for transferring people whose technical skills are indispensable, but whose management potential is non-existent, to some place where they're not going to alienate all your staff. Start at the top and set about *managing* the changes. Some of them *can* be made to happen.

Management Recruitment and Selection Policy

Here's another truism: *management selection should take account of the style or profile that the organization's needs dictate.* Maybe it *does* take such account – but since I know quite a few organizations where any assertion that it did would need the rider 'but not all that much', here are some considerations about management selection and recruitment:

Write and publish a recruitment policy

Publish some guidelines which reflect the true values of the organization and ensure that all decision-takers have a copy of it and understand what it says.

Check the recruit's track record/potential

Are the 'key elements' of style present? How can you tell? What's been achieved in the past? Can the deficiencies be supplemented or trained out?

Do you need to recruit what the job spec says?

Who wrote the job specification or person specification anyhow? *Why* do you need to recruit a 21-year-old male graduate? Who else could do this job?

Think outside the square

Try to be creative in your thinking. Does the job have to be filled by a man? Or a woman? Why? What about ethnic groups? Are you *really* an equal opportunities employer or do you simply ensure you employ your statutory quota?

Watch out for the 'halo' effect

It is a well-known tendency for managers to recruit people who are like themselves. This, of course, can be good or bad news. Often it's bad, because nobody really knows themselves. Too many managers look for a number of superficially attractive attributes which don't stand up to the test of time.

Insist that senior managers own the process

Don't do it for them! Make senior managers own the process *right from the word go*. This means they should offer the job, write the letter and plan the induction and training process – with your help maybe, but don't allow them to 'cop out'.

Stamp out prejudice and discrimination

Don't turn a blind eye and say you disapprove. Report it and stamp on it hard. Prejudice is bad business – it costs reputations and money.

Induction

Management induction is more important in business terms than anybody else's induction because the values that you're able to instil in the first six months of a manager's career with you, will stay with him or her for a very long time. Of course, if you get it wrong, all the potential impact will be lost. So ensure that the issues that are important to your organization are taught early.

Management style and selection are going to become more important than ever in the 90s. It is, therefore, vital that managers should understand modern values and the realities of today's socio-economic climate. At the moment, there is a very long way to go. An independent opinion poll conducted by Gallup in May 1990 shows that:

> 90 per cent of British employers discriminate against over-35s as being too old.
>
> 30 per cent of British companies still prefer under-25s.
>
> most employers reject over-50s as having 'insufficent stamina and being set in their ways'. 86 per cent of employers prefer to recruit under 35s.
>
> 90 per cent of employers recognize there will be a shortfall of school leavers – but two-thirds are taking *no action at all.*

Chapter 6
When Supervisors Hold the Key

Introduction

Tinsley Bridge Ltd used to be part of the British Steel Corporation, until, in a management buy-out, a group of its managers acquired the ownership of this traditional Sheffield Steel manufacturer, which makes springs for the automotive industry.

They quickly realized that keen market competition was placing demands upon the company which simply weren't being met. New standards were needed, not just in manufacturng quality, but also in volume, delivery and, above all, value for money. And in the new 'private' world, failure would carry a real penalty which could no longer be hidden in the accounts of a large corporation

At the same time, Tinsley Bridge also had to face traditional problems. Change had not easily been achieved in the steel industry where people were used to driving hard bargains and where hearts and minds are not easily won. Disputes and disagreements were part of the fabric. The concept of 'total quality' was foreign to many employees and managers, except for a handful of visionaries who could see what might be possible if only attitudes could be changed.

But whose attitudes? The unions? The employees? Everybody's? And where did you start? Was there some kind of blueprint you could transfer?

Sensibly enough, Tinsley Bridge decided to take advice. They took a close look at a number of British organizations which had embarked on the same journey as the one they were contemplating. One major influence was to be found in Nissan UK. TBL invited Peter Wickens, its Personnel Director to come and take part in a management conference at all levels including first line supervisors.

Wickens is a pragmatist. Originally a product of the Ford Motor Company, he was manager of industrial relations at Dagenham and had later started up the Continental Can Company on a green site in North Wales. He knows more than most people about change –

how people resist it and why; and what the key ingredients are to achieving it. He passionately believes in the role of the first line manager in communicating and leading the improvement process. But he also knows very well that the key to managing change is leadership – and that employees can't be effectively led unless the *climate* for leadership is right.

Wickens pointed out that whatever else Tinsley Bridge did, three factors were crucial:

Everyone had to 'buy into' the vision. Yet this would never be possible if people believed that there was one law for the rich and another for the poor. In other words, some people were seen to be unfairly advantaged to the detriment of others.

Deeds were more important than words. Tinsley Bridge couldn't simply *talk* about treating everyone fairly – there had to be positive action. Harmonization, justice being seen to be done, equality of opportunity – all had to be practiced and not just preached.

Supervisors were the crucial link. All Wicken's experience showed that if things were not right at this level, nothing happened at all. And, according to the supervisors, things *weren't* right at this level. They felt undermined, badly supported and less well informed than the shop stewards who had more influence.

All of this left a great impression on three key players on the Tinsley Bridge Board: the Chairman, Michael Webber, Production Director, David Roberts, and Personnel Director, Terry Steel. It would be wrong to imply that it was an experience to be compared with the Road to Damascus. But as Dave Roberts pointed out: 'Nobody had really put into words so effectively what we'd felt for a long time.'

As a result, the decision was taken that Tinsley Bridge, in order to start becoming a total quality company, would:

- Implement a harmonization policy (in order to eliminate un-fairness and injustice)
- Change the status of its foremen and turn them into respected members of the management team
- Train and develop managers to respond to the new demands that Tinsley Bridge would place upon them.

(My company, Sargent Minton Lennon Ltd was retained to advise on the implementation of the policy and design and carry out an appropriate training programme. This article, which first appeared in *Works Management,* is an independent review of what has happened subsequently.)

Case Study – Tinsley Bridge Ltd.

The background

In 1989 senior managers at Tinsley Bridge Limited (TBL) made a bargain with their supervisors.

The significance of this bargain for TBL is bound up in the complex recent history of the company. In the summer of 1987, Tinsley Bridge, then part of the British Steel Corporation (BSC), was bought out by its management. The buy-out followed five dark years of retrenchment and rationalization in which the company had survived by adopting an aggressive, high profile management style designed to shake out the air of complacency which, until then, had characterized workforce attitudes.

It was a stormy period of change. The company's elaborate and individual incentive schemes were streamlined. Discipline was tightened. Monthly communication meetings between management and workforce were set up. And a 'total quality' philosophy was introduced.

Sporadically, workforce resentment boiled over into industrial action. Yet slowly, the realization that radical change was both inevitable and necessary began to permeate through to the shop-floor and this was reflected in improved productivity backed by a steady growth in orders.

It was in this environment of growing confidence that Tinsley Bridge's management, led by Michael Webber and backed by 3i Plc, bought the company from BSC in July 1987. A year later, 95 per cent of employees took the opportunity of buying shares amounting to some 8 per cent of the company. Webber now considered the time was ripe for management to attempt its most ambitious change to date.

TBL's on-going campaign to remove all unnecessary barriers in the company (for instance, between functions, and between operators and craftsmen) culminated on 1 April 1989, in a company-wide move to single-status staff conditions. From that date, instead of clocking-in, changing for work and going to their machines, employees would simply arrive ready for work at a particular time and each team would meet together to start the shift correctly.

Under such conditions, first-line supervisors would have to play a pivotal role. They would need to lead and brief each team on each shift and take a large measure of responsibility for employee attendance and discipline. They would be expected to run each section as a business in its own right, ensure that effective maintenance was performed, maintain high quality standards under a new Statistical Process Control regime and still perform the day-to-day duties of a supervisor. Says Webber: 'If it didn't work at their level, it didn't work at all.'

The problem was, TBL's supervisors were not prepared. Indeed, when single-status working was first suggested in October 1988, the supervisors had already been struggling to adapt to changing working practices introduced since 1982. Recalls Webber: 'The company was moving fast. The order load was developing rapidly; people-development aspects were running in parallel with total quality; we were having courses throughout the works, and in the middle of all this, the supervisors were being asked for more. They were a bit mesmerized.'

The speed of change was also placing considerable strain on the relationship between management and supervisors, as David Roberts, Operations Director, recalls: 'They were resenting the pressure on them to manage in a different way. We were trying to move the company at a pace they found very uncomfortable.'

At about this time time, Roberts attended a seminar at Nissan, which enjoys considerable success with team working, single status and supervisor development. There, each shift starts with a short meeting, led by the supervisor, in meeting rooms designed for that purpose. A question and answer session follows an update on the day's problems, then everybody begins work having been properly briefed.

Says Webber: 'Our supervisors needed to be able to lead and run their teams in that way. We then said: "That will never happen unless we give them the necessary training and provide the facilities and the system which makes it occur normally and naturally".' Physically, that simply meant constructing meeting rooms on the shopfloor where each team could start the shift. Mentally, it required a great leap forward by supervisors.

Culture change

TBL's supervisors needed to make a culture change. They needed to see the logic of the proposed working method and understand their place within it. But, primarily, they had to recognize their own importance and take responsibility for making the change. Webber is emphatic on this point: 'Time and time again we came to the view that the action takes place at first-line supervisor level, and if that was weak we were wasting our time with the other initiatives. It was vital they saw themselves as managers – and, what is more, *as the critical point of management that makes things happen.'*

With this objective in mind, a seminar was arranged for all the supervisors in which *they* were left to define what their role should be. After more than a day of discussion the supervisors reached a definition which closely matched the role envisaged by TBL's managers. It was a real breakthrough. Says Webber: 'If we'd just told them what we wanted, it would not have worked. They had to *own* that definition for themselves.'

Ultimately, this consensus laid the foundation of the bargain between managers and supervisors. This was the deal: TBL would provide training to help supervisors learn the style and approach needed for the future. They would be given all the opportunities and support necessary for that new role and assume the title of 'section manager'. In return, the supervisors had to give their wholehearted commitment to new working practices and, where necessary, give up their own time for training.

Explains Webber: 'There was obviously a stick and carrot i.e. we'll provide the training but you've got to make the grade. If you're good enough you'll be better rewarded, have a new title and know that you've got the whole management team supporting you. But yes, there is a risk.'

It was agreed that if anybody could *not* give their commitment or was unable to reach the necessary standard, they would be moved to a different position on existing terms and conditions.

Both sides were relieved that positive action was being taken to resolve the deadlock developing between senior managers and supervisors. Roberts recalls: 'It was getting to the stage where I wasn't going to back off and they weren't going to surrender and after a while we both became a little tired of the whole situation. But the minute the new role was agreed, it was as if something locked up inside them had broken out. Some immediately discarded the traditional supervisors' smock, came to work in a suit and started managing in a different way. They'd made a mental and physical change.'

The next step was to devise a training programme. A consultancy was commissioned to work out a training syllabus derived from detailed conversations with the management team and each of the supervisors. Nine modules were developed to suit the needs of the TBL section managers (former supervisors), which could be re-shaped as the training progressed. These are described briefly on page 53.

Initial training sessions commenced at the end of October 1988, were held on Sundays, and lasted all day. Training certainly wasn't a new experience for the section managers – most had attended quite extensive training when TBL was part of British Steel. But, as Webber points out, the BSC courses were intended to create a good foreman in an ideal environment. They never took account of the far from normal environment that the supervisors were returning to after training; the emphasis was on discipline and 'getting it done' rather than leading a team.

A team effort

The initial TBL sessions were a great success. Says Webber: 'They were all a bit worried at first but they stayed together as a team and, having decided it was going to happen, they were keen that it should be right. From that point on, they variously had doubts and were very enthusiastic depending on the stage in the training. But no-one said: "This is not for me".'

Training as a team brought other benefits, as Terry Steel, Personnel Director, explains: 'Going through the modules as a group allowed them to relate to each other's experiences.' A lot, too, depended on the consultant being seen as a friend of both sides. Says Webber: 'I don't believe we could have done the training ourselves and achieved the same effect. The open and honest relationship between trainer and section managers helped to make it all gel.'

When 1 April finally arrived, a group of very apprehensive super-visors stood up in front of their single status teams, briefed them ready for the day's work and started the shift. Nobody would say the men were 100 per cent ready but, says Webber: 'The initial training did a good enough job for them to realize they must give it their best shot. Without exception, they all believed in what they were doing that morning.'

Since then, the scheme has been operating very successfully. For Section Manager, Brian Hobson and his colleagues, the old 'super-visor' role is hardly recognizable. Much of the day-to-day work –

scheduling and paperwork – is delegated to chargehands, who also
deputize in their section managers' absence. Says Hobson: 'There's
far more time for appraisals, people management and organizing
training. I was one of the sceptics – if someone had said that a year
from now chargehands would be doing my job, I wouldn't have
believed them.'

This policy of downward delegation and increased flexibility is
extending to the entire workforce and falls firmly within the section
manager's remit. He or she must oversee the entire SPC (Statistical
Process Control) scheme on the shop-floor. Maintenance and production functions have been brought together under one operation,
widening the section manager's sphere of influence to craftsmen
and technicians as well as production operatives.

More specific training for section managers, some of it one-to-
one, is currently under way to prepare them for these changes. This,
and the considerable amount of operative training needed to establish SPC, has prompted TBL to invest in a permanent on-site
training centre, a facility which, says Webber, 'We desperately
need.'

Building for the future

Tinsley Bridge is beginning to be successful. Profits are up, order
books are healthy, capital expenditure is increasing. The workforce
is growing, people are confident. The supervisor initiative has made
a significant contribution, but everybody agrees, they've only just
begun. Says Operations Manager, Tony Buxton: 'If we stop looking
for improvement in our section managers' skills, the business will
stop progressing. There's a long way to go.'

Webber sums up the fundamental importance of supervisor development: 'The idea of leadership had got lost along the way. They
did not see their role as leading, helping, developing and defending
their people. They saw it as doing what management told them to
do. We *had* to do something about that. They are the cornerstone to
all we're trying to achieve.'

Appendix: the TBL section manager development programme

Following the interviews and assessment of training needs carried
out by the consultancy, nine modules were developed tailored
specifically to TBL's requirements. Most modules include on- and
off-the-job project work:

- The role of the section manager as a leader – aiming to develop *self-awareness* in the art of leadership
- Communications skills – including verbal and written presentation, leading a briefing group and using presentation equipment
- Industrial relations – covering discipline and grievance procedures, employment legislation, health and safety regulations and communicating with shop stewards
- Financial management – giving section managers an understanding of the financial objectives of the business and their contribution
- Personnel management – this module aims to develop skills in counselling, guidance and personal problem solving as well as to prepare the section manager for recruiting and handling absenteeism
- Instructional techniques – aims to enhance the section manager's on-the-job training function, especially in the areas of quality and cost control
- Quality management – to ensure full understanding of the concept of Total Quality Management, Statistical Process Control and compliance with BS5750.
- Production and inventory management – covering JIT (Just In Time), economic batch scheduling and improved stock control
- Engineering aspects – covering planned maintenance and the impact of product development on the section manager's role.

Conclusion

The programme which Tinsley Bridge followed, was successful, measured by virtually any standards. Productivity, volume, manufacturing quality, cost-effectiveness, have all improved significantly – and, of course, success leads to success. But this is not the place to blow trumpets – the important issues to remember and discuss about the Tinsley Bridge experience are these:

1 *Leadership from the front*
The TBL Board has demonstrated throughout its commitment to the TBL programme by investing real time, effort, and money.

2 *Keeping faith*
Tinsley Bridge has kept its promises. The training *was* done. The

promotions for foremen *were* made. Support *is* provided. Harmonization *has* happened. Nobody has been 'economical with the truth.'

3   *Planning change*
Tinsley Bridge planned the whole change process over a period of months. There were few open-ended commitments.

4   *Participation*
The employees were sufficiently impressed by the honesty and directness of the management approach to join in, take part, and let facts judge the effectiveness.

5   *Consultancy help*
Tinsley was wise in its use of consultancy advice. It followed the first two rules for using consultants well: choose someone you like and take the advice you're offered. (The third rule says: 'If you don't like the advice, get rid of the consultant.')

Chapter 7
Harmonizing Terms and Conditions of Employment

'I've worked in this factory for more than fifteen years; I am an instrument fitter on the highest grade; when I come to work, I have to go in the back entrance, change into overalls and clock in. When I have my mid-day break I eat in the factory canteen. I am "hourly paid", I get my money in cash in an envelope every Friday; if I go sick I get just the Government's Sick Benefit. Now my daughter has just left school to work in the sales office. She goes in the front door, she eats in the staff restaurant; she gets an annual salary, paid monthly by cheque; she starts work later than me, she's on the company sick-pay scheme, she doesn't have to clock in. It gets up my nose.'

Twenty years ago, this sort of complaint would have been commonplace. Nowadays, happily, there are few companies where you will come across status differences as wide and as numerous as this; during the past fifteen or so years, quite a number of distinctions between blue and white collars have been eliminated. Indeed, now that we are coming towards the end of the twentieth century, one might have thought that the argument for harmonization was so powerful that it really did not require much further debate.

What is Harmonization?

The traditional definition is something along the following lines:

'Harmonization is the achievement of common terms and conditions of employment for manual and non-manual workers in the organization.'

ACAS have defined it as: 'the narrowing or elimination of the differences in the basis of treatment of manual and non-manual workers regarding pay, fringe benefits and other conditions of employment' (ACAS Occasional Paper, No. 41: *Labour Flexibility in Britain.*) I shall argue further on, however, for a slightly different definition of the term.

The Past

In our industrial past, the treatment of people at work as two different social classes probably seemed the natural way of things. It was no doubt believed that this was an essential device for the system to work effectively. And so, with the exception of a handful of philanthropists, employers maintained a strict division between the working and the middle classes.

Nineteenth-century laws designed to protect workmen did nothing to encourage progress towards single status. For example, the Truck Acts of 1830 required that workmen had to be paid in cash, but made no such restriction for managers and white-collar workers, whose rewards could partly be in terms of fringe benefits. These Acts were originally designed to protect employees of canal and railway builders from having to receive their pay in vouchers which could only be exchanged for goods provided by the employer. So the practice of the manual worker receiving his or her pay in the form of cash in a pay packet was created. And even today – because you may not unilaterally alter the method of payment – companies have sometimes had difficulty in persuading employees to accept 'cashless pay'.

Gradual Change

Some say that the change towards single status started late and is proceeding all too slowly. New industries and technologies have made such distinctions seem ever more outdated.

An important early factor was the incomes policies imposed by successive governments from the Second World War to the end of the 1970s in their attempts to combat inflation. Because you could often get round these legitimately by agreeing non-cash benefits, trade unions turned increasingly to bargaining for some of the benefits enjoyed hitherto only by white-collar workers.

Moves towards harmonization of terms and conditions often make economic sense. The costs of providing both canteens and of paying cash, have led to single-status eating arrangements and to 'cashless pay' for all. Companies that have adopted flexible working hours – or 'flexitime' – have made savings by harmonizing their methods of recording working hours.

Such economic arguments have been made even stronger by the decline in the proportion of traditional blue-collar workers in the country's workforce. It has become relatively less costly to harmonize terms and conditions when in many companies the 'hourly paid' make up only a minority of the total employed.

Employees' Views of Status Differences

Employees' views of 'privileges' enjoyed by white-collar workers are not necessarily negative. I suspect these differences are more common in the so-called 'traditional' industries, where it has been the custom for people to stay for their whole working lives and to work their way up the ladder, perhaps crossing the 'blue-white' barrier when they become supervisors.

In such circumstances, companies engaged in harmonization programmes sometimes encounter resistance from white-collar employees attempting to maintain their differentials: 'I've worked up to this level, and I'm not giving up my fitted carpet without a struggle.' For others, the eventual prospect of gaining the 'fitted carpet' or its equivalent may be a motivator, and you need to take these feelings into account when deciding on your policy.

Changing from 'hourly pay' to 'salary' can also meet resistance. People at work may feel that whilst they are hourly paid, they have better control over their earnings, especially if pay can be enhanced, for example, by voluntary overtime. Such fears of loss of control can lead people to fight what to management might appear to be obvious improvements.

Outdated working practices and demarcations frequently accompany 'unharmonized' terms and conditions. This means that in older industries harmonization may involve major cultural change and managers may be surprised by the opposition to some of their proposals. They might meet with cynical responses like: 'You're all calling us "staff" now so you can keep our wages down' or 'You're putting us on salaries so you can do away with overtime.'

Even when status differences have been officially abolished, people sometimes choose to maintain them for themselves. I recall going to the restaurant in a progressive company which had gone a long way down the harmonization road. As I came off the end of the self-service queue to put my tray down on a particular table, the training manager said: 'Don't sit there, that's where the MD sits!' In the same company, somebody said to me: 'I have my boss breathing down my neck all day. The last thing I want to do is have lunch with him.'

It is not just the differences between white- and blue-collar workers which cause problems. In industries such as banking and insurance, which employ comparatively few blue collars, it was traditional for people to 'earn' privileges as they climbed the ladder. Yet here too social and technological changes have led to more harmonization. It is rare now to find 'services' staff on different pensions, holidays, payment methods and allowances.

A New Definition?

I believe it is now time to expand the definition of harmonization to include the reduction/elimination of all *unnecessary* differences between employees, not just the differences between blue- and white-collar workers. This distinction is becoming increasingly blurred, anyway – many of the new industries are, if anything, 'white coat'. Managers and employees would find the terms 'blue collar' and 'white collar' almost incomprehensible, yet some irritating and unnecessary status differences are still maintained.

'Unnecessary' is the key word, of course, yet people have different views on what that means. What is an unnecessary difference in one industry may be accepted in another. This does not mean to say that 'We've always had it' or 'We've always done it this way' should go unchallenged.

You may, however, have some differences in the treatment of people which, on the face of it, seem to be unnecessary but are important for the efficient running of the business. You may have a policy on company cars for your sales force which ensures that their vehicles are as impressive as those of your competitors. In organizations such as the armed services, the police, the emergency services and perhaps security firms, it *is* important to be able to recognize who's in charge. To put everybody in the same uniform, without distinctions, is superficially attractive and certainly provides a symbolic sense of single status, but it won't work everywhere.

You may also have a policy of providing different terms and conditions at the top of the managerial scale. There may well be good business reasons, such as the need to be competitive in recruiting and retaining top people, for maintaining them.

Yet many *irrelevant* status differences still remain. They are insidious, create jealousies and damage morale. They frequently waste an inordinate amount of management time, and all too often they go hand in hand with restrictive working practices and outdated attitudes.

> A civil servant – a Higher Executive Officer – was moved into an office previously occupied by a Senior Executive Officer. The office was provided with a wall-to-wall carpet. A few days later, a man came in, armed with a large pair of carpet shears. 'Sorry, guv, I'm afraid you're not entitled to a fitted carpet.' He then proceeded to crawl round the perimeter of the room, cutting a strip of eighteen inches off the carpet.

Such absurd differences between grades are completely out of touch with modern working practices.

What about the 'company car'? Many employees have one for business purposes, as well as private use, as part of their contract of employment. Usually there is a policy, or tariff, laying down what sort of car you are entitled to, according to your position or grade in the organization. Because of the importance of the car as a status symbol, company-car policies cause argument and contention and a considerable waste of management time in effecting them. Companies have even had to devise rules for what extras employees may put on their cars at their own expense. I am not arguing that you should abolish company cars, but in most organizations they could probably do with some harmonization.

Harmonizing Your Terminology

Some organizations don't have employees. They use terms like partners, members or associates instead. All expressions of a wish for harmony. I even know a company which, in wishing to achieve a feeling of togetherness, doesn't like to use the word 'management' to describe, well – the management. You might think that's taking things a bit far, and might serve to confuse people, especially new employees.

In principle, there is nothing wrong in wishing to harmonize your terminology, but beware! If you call your employees 'partners' but impose unnecessary differences between the white-collar and blue-collar workers, the likely result will be cynicism at best!

Why Harmonize?

Here are some of the main reasons:

Economic factors

Differences are costly and wasteful – and there's a tendency for governments to increase tax on fringe benefits, anyway. If we harmonize, we can simplify our wage negotiations and our terms and conditions in general.

Harmonization can often help us to offer a more competitive reward package. We have to compete for an ever declining number of young people. We're running out of teenagers. They won't put up with the traditional 'junior's' jobs, and we can't afford to employ them in such jobs either. Harmonization between age groups is as important as harmonization between other groups.

Employee relations

Differences are divisive; they are unfair and unjust. The days when the skilled worker's young daughter enjoyed better terms of employment than he did are surely over. If we harmonize, we will improve our industrial relations. Sometimes the employees put pressure on us to eliminate unnecessary differences. Harmonization will also help to improve motivation and team spirit. Single status at work is the trend.

Greenfield Sites

If you are starting from scratch, single status makes sense. Everybody has heard stories, and a few exaggerated ones too, about the way Japanese companies are managed in the UK – everybody wearing the same uniform, everybody on exactly the same terms and conditions, with salary being the only difference. The intention of the management is to build a unified workforce, a team all pulling in the same direction. On the industrial relations front, 'single union' agreements, 'single-table bargaining' and structures which facilitate two-way communication are all part of the scheme, and help to set the pace towards harmonization.

Clearly, irrelevant distinctions are not in accord with this philosophy. If you are setting up a new firm, now's the chance to make sure unnecessary differences do not exist.

It Is Not All Smooth Sailing

There are some managerial benefits that are not in line with modern working practices. It is unfair, for example, to have a 'no alcohol at work' rule at the same time as a well-stocked cocktail cabinet in the managers' dining room. (It is not good for efficiency either.)

When is a difference 'unacceptable'? Differences between locations may become as big a bone of contention in the future as differences between grades have been. There is still a strong trend towards decentralized pay settlements. With less emphasis on national agreements, employers have more flexibility than hitherto. Watch out, however, that your use of today's new-found flexibility does not lead to tomorrow's unacceptable differences.

It is fashionable (and makes economic sense, for example, to try for different pay rates between the North and the South. Now the state of the labour market in the South, particularly in the South-East, may justify such differences – but where do you draw the boundary? How happy will the people be who live on just the wrong side of such a boundary? Organizations with London Allowances – sometimes separate Central, Inner, and Outer London Allowances – are *constantly* faced with claims for boundaries to be changed or for special cases to be considered.

What Gets Harmonized?

The following categories of terms and conditions may be helpful:

Pay and Grading
Grading structure
Calculation of pay
Method of payment
Bonuses
Profit share/share purchase schemes

Working Time
Basic weekly hours
Total basic holidays
Service-related holidays
Holiday pay calculation
Special (e.g. bereavement) leave
Timing/flexibility of hours
Timing/flexibility of holidays
Recording attendance
Overtime
Shift premia

Income Security
Sick leave
Sick pay
Redundancy pay
Occupational pension
Health insurance

Other Conditions
Canteen/restaurant
Car parking
Loans
Luncheon vouchers
Travel expenses
Product discounts

Nothing in the terms and conditions need be automatically ruled out, and the trend in the past ten years or so has been for considerable harmonization in holidays, redundancy pay arrangements, pensions, canteen/restaurant facilities, staff purchase discounts and car parking. There seems to have been less advance in pay systems, grading structures, hours of work and methods of recording attendance.

A recent survey *(IRS Employment Trends Survey,* August/ November 1989) states that companies gave the following motives for harmonization, in order of preference:

To remove unjustifiable barriers etc. – 33 mentions
To simplify negotiations/terms and conditions – 16 mentions
To enhance motivation/team spirit, etc. – 9 mentions
To provide a more competitive package – 8 mentions
To improve industrial relations – 5 mentions
To respond to pressure from trade unions – 4 mentions
To avoid leap-frogging claims – 2 mentions
To pre-empt union demands – 1 mention
To reduce the likelihood of union recognition – 1 mention
To ease the introduction of new technology – 1 mention

The IRS Survey also states that the initiative for harmonization generally comes from the employer, and it is followed by a greater degree of joint activity after the initial phase. There's no evidence to suggest that non-union companies are keener on harmonization than unionized ones, nor that it is the preserve of the new or 'greenfield' sites. The vast majority of agreements on harmonization are concluded as part of a package deal during the normal pay negotiations. Only a few are arrangements introduced as a separate package.

How To Do It

You probably cannot reduce or eliminate all your 'unacceptable differences' at a stroke. Apart from the cost, you are frequently asking people to accept significant cultural changes, so go from step to step:

Step 1: Review where you are now. Examine everything relating to terms and conditions. The list of what gets harmonized given above covers most matters that *could* be harmonized.

Ask yourself:
1. Is the difference essential for the efficient running of the business?
2. Is it important for the maintenance of good, productive employee relations?
3. Does it motivate people to produce their best?
4. Is it cheaper to keep it than to eliminate it?

If you can say 'no' to *any* of these questions, then it's time to *consider* eliminating the difference in question.

Step 2: Work out where you would like to be, in the long, medium and short terms – and be *realistic*.

Step 3: Share your thoughts with everybody and ask for their views. Discuss it with all your managers, and put the subject on the agenda of your consultative committees, backed with clear supporting information.

Step 4: Having consulted, work out your priorities and plans. If you negotiate with trade unions, always link improvements to terms and conditions with your pay strategy.

Phase in your harmonization plans. You probably cannot do it all at once. Remember, most harmonization is 'upward' and can cost you money.

Chapter 8
Harmonization Works

Dennis Ruabon Ltd is a 'traditional' manufacturer of ceramic products. Based in Ruabon, near Wrexham in North Wales, it is privately owned and will almost inevitably continue to be so. Everything it manufacturers comes out of a hole in the ground a few yards down the road – and has done for a century. In fact this has been true for hundreds of years as, since time immemorial, Ruabon has boasted a manufacturer in ceramics on this site. It currently employs 180 people and in 1988 had a turnover of £6.2 million.

Many values in the clay industry are pretty traditional too. It has not been easy to modernize the industry. Reject and waste rates have always been high, and the industry has had difficulty in producing an image consistent with modern manufacturing and trading standards.

When John Troth joined the company at the end of the 1980s, it was clear that change had to be made. High absenteeism, low productivity, inadequate volume together with marketing and customer service problems, all meant that as Managing Director he had to take initiatives which would decide whether or not Dennis Ruabon could both survive and compete. And while it was clear that some capital investment was required, the fact remained that unless attitudes could be changed, Dennis Ruabon wasn't going anywhere except downhill.

Troth had previously been Production Director at Westbrick, which had been an independent brick manufacturer and is now part of the Tarmac Group. He is also a visionary with an intense and keen sense of fairness, and, it must be said, a natural leader and campaigner. So he was obviously aggrieved – even insulted – to be presiding over a 13 per cent absentee rate, and a less than enviable industrial relations record. There was also a raft of manufacturing, engineering and sales inadequacies, many of which were as much the product of human error and omission as they were the result of old fashioned methods, or lack of capital investment.

Clearly something had to be done.

The Turning of the Tide . . .

By the late 1970s, the company faced great competitive pressure and was in need of capital investment to update existing production methods (tiles were still being made by traditional craft methods involving beehive kilns). In 1979, a dispute erupted, with hourly-paid workers walking out after forklift truck drivers were promised an 'off-the-cuff' increase of £5 per week. The dispute highlighted the poor union organization and the disparity between rates of pay for piece-rate workers operating the kilns and those such as sorters and packers on hourly rates of pay. The existing piece-rate system encouraged productivity at the expense of quality, with wastage levels of 30-50 per cent (see Table 1).

In the wake of the dispute, a survey and report by ACAS highlighted key shortcomings in working conditions and pay structures: absenteeism was high, union representation effectively non-existent, and no formal industrial relations procedures or structures were present. The need for greater training of managers at all levels was also identified. Implementing the recommendations of the ACAS report, together with management inititiatives since, has provided much of the foundation on which the success of Dennis Ruabon in the last decade has been built.

Table 1
Some of the key indicators of change at Denis Ruabon 1978-88

	1978	1988
Turnover	£2.4m	£6.2m
Pre-tax profit	7.1%	9.4%
Number employed	268	180
Product range	Quarry tiles	Quarry tiles and clay pavers, multi-coloured and multi-shaped
Wastage levels	30-50%	10%
Pay levels	54	5 job-evaluated grades, plus a supervisor grade
Absenteeism	10-25%	Less than 3%

Trade Union Participation

In the wake of the 1979 dispute, a recognition agreement was signed with the Transport and General Workers' Union (TGWU). A Steering Committee was set up to formulate discipline and grievance procedures, devise consultative meetings and new pay structures, plan training for managers, supervisors and shop stewards, and carry out job evaluation for shopfloor employees. This committee comprised company directors, the Personnel Manager, the Union Branch Chairman and Secretary, a Union district official and an ACAS representative. The committee was later to become the Company Joint Council, to which the Joint Consultative Committee and Health and Safety Committee reported.

One of its first jobs was to rationalize the pay structure system – at the time of the dispute 54 pay levels were in operation! Five pay levels were established and determined by job evaluation. In 1983/4, after installation of the new plant, a redundancy agreement was negotiated between management and union with 85 employees leaving on a 'last in, first out' basis. Then moves were made towards harmonization between shopfloor employees and office staff.

Harmonization

In the words of Brian Reader, the Personnel Manager, this has been a case of 'the art of the possible'. Close co-operation between management and union has enabled phased improvement in employee terms and conditions (see Table 2). 1988 saw the culmination of 5 years' progress towards harmonization: the staff and works employees now have a single Contract of Employment and benefits package.

Table 2
Countdown to Harmonization

March 1984	Shopfloor employees no longer clock on
October 1984	All wages paid by bank transfer
November 1984	Sickness benefit of 25% paid from first day of sickness
April 1985	Pension contributions increased from 3 to 4%. Company sick pay increased from 25 to 50% of basic pay
April 1986	Pension raised from 4 to 5%
April 1987	Hours of work reduced from 42 to 41 hours without production loss
July 1987	Fortnightly pay begins; company sick pay increased from 50 to 75% of basic pay
January 1988	Company sick pay increased from 75 to 100% of basic pay (includes Statutory Sick Pay)
April 1988	Hours of work reduced from 41 to 39.5 hours per week without production loss; monthly pay for all; pension schemes merged; shopfloor and office staff now share same Contract of Employment and benefits package

Communications

The company tries to be as open as possible; employees find out about current developments through a monthly briefing with their first-line manager. A monthly briefing statement is produced by the senior management, while other items of news and information are incorporated in an occasional company news-sheet. Noticeboards are now used to give information on departmental performance, absenteeism rates, and product quality and quantity. Much of the flow of information from employees to managers comes via shop stewards through regular weekly meetings.

Technological Developments

The improved industrial-relations climate enabled capital to be borrowed and in 1982/3 a major capital investment of £3.5 million was undertaken to build a new plant adjacent to the original factory. This utilizes recent technology in extruded tile manufacture developed in Germany and incorporates some of the most modern extrusion, handling and firing equipment available in the world.

Alongside this, new packaging and palletization systems were developed to improve distribution and presentation of products to the customer. In 1985, a further major investment in a modern, high-speed, technically controlled shuttle kiln enabled almost continuous kiln operation.

Management and Training

The company (working with Sargent Minton Ltd as consultants) had recognized that, to support the initiatives taken on the technological front, the skill and expertise of managers at every level needed developing to:

- Enable them to manage in a changing environment
- Be innovative enough to introduce new initiatives when needed
- Improve two-way communication between employees and themselves
- Understand and implement changes in working methods.

Senior management training took place between 1982 and 1986. In 1986, first-line managers (ie supervisors) were targeted as the vital link with employees. The MSC was approached to approve and part-fund a Managing Company Expansion (MACE) programme for supervisors. With the programme agreed, meetings were held by the training consultants with supervisors and their respective managers to identify weaknesses and to formulate a 16-day modular programme (spread over 7 months) covering Leadership, Communications, Interviewing, Negotiating, Financial and Business Management, Stores Management, Purchasing Techniques, Computers, Health and Safety, Clay Technology and Quality Assurance, and Managing Terms and Conditions of Employment.

The training, which was largely participative, used a wide variety of approaches, including role play, case studies, team exercises and the use of video and audiotapes and demonstrations of computer applications. The main outcome was a new kind of supervisor, able to take on, and indeed demanding, managerial responsibility.

On-the-job training is undertaken with all new shopfloor employees, and a matrix checklist is kept of their training experiences. The aim is to produce a well-rounded, flexible workforce, able to change roles to meet the demands of new and urgent orders, while also enhancing the variety and interest in the work.

The Quality Improvement Programme

Dennis Ruabon is committed to developing a philosophy of Total Quality Management throughout the company. In 1989, Dennis began work with first-line and middle managers in raising awareness of the key concepts of TQM and jointly devising a training programme which managers could use with their staff. The aim is to enable managers, working with shopfloor staff in teams, to analyse tasks, set standards, identify faults, solve problems and facilitate 'continual improvement'. Two such working groups – one examining the problem of 'tile distortion' and the other 'shade control' – have been operating very successfully from mid-1989. The eventual aim is for all employees to be operating from the 'internal customer' concept, aware of each job task and its specific quality standards.

The Pay-off

Dennis Ruabon isn't the Garden of Eden. It isn't a bright shiny new company bristling with boffins and technology. On the contrary, it's a traditional old firm set in the middle of rural Wales. It's cold, draughty, occasionally leaky and certainly a bit dirty and dusty. After all, it processes clay! What it has done in the past ten years is to recognize that people who work in such conditions have feelings too. It's recognized that motivation has to be *managed* – with sense and sensitivity – and the rewards have been immense.

Flexibility

Dennis Ruabon has achieved a degree of flexibility from its workforce that some observers would have considered impossible. The fact is, however, that a significant number of employees can satisfactorily (and willingly) perform different duties and there is great flexibility with regard to working hours and practices.

Quality

The company is improving its quality record all the time. Reject rates are being cut. BS5750 was achieved early and products are competing strongly in world markets (as they have to).

Behaviour

Strikes don't happen. Absenteeism is down to around 3 per cent and to any observer the working climate is clearly harmonious.

The Future

The clay industry isn't easy. Its image is not consistent with its aspirations and with the expectations of many potential employees. Furthermore, it's very competitive – and there are numerous smaller outlets where quality and price differentials can be achieved more cost-effectively. This obviously puts pressure on firms like Dennis Ruabon – and this has been exacerbated in the last few years by high interest rates and high exchange rates which have inflated costs and depressed sales at the same time. Yet Dennis has survived all of this and improved its ability to compete by:

- Changing both behaviour and attitudes at all levels
- Improving industrial relations beyond all recognition
- Achieving better value for money by improving its pay and rewards systems
- Training and developing managers
- Improving communications
- Introducing a policy of Total Quality Management

Many personnel managers are understandably and often rightly, influenced by the experience of such companies as IBM, Nissan, Marks and Spencer, British Airways, etc. Frequently, such organizations seem out of reach and difficult to copy. Yet the experience of Dennis Ruabon shows that, given the right quality of leadership and sensible objectives, personnel standards and motivation can be improved and built upon even in small, comparatively unsophisticated companies.

It's all a question of being able to see where you want to be and then leading a systematic and determined campaign to ensure that you get there.

Chapter 9
Managing Performance

Performance and Reward

Pay and rewards are subjects for a book all on their own. However, it cannot make sense to write about performance management without some reference to reward.

First of all, let's not confuse 'reward' with recognition. What many people seek from work is *fair* payment. The 1976 survey by the CBI into attitudes and understanding showed that nearly 70 per cent of workpeople expect a *fair* day's pay for a *fair* day's work. No research before or since has seriously questioned this. So it would be wrong to assume that achievement *necessarily* warrants extra monetary reward. However, what they also seek from work is *recognition* and that means they want to feel that someone appreciates what they do. Saying 'thank you' is a very good start.

Recognition can take many forms: a letter, for example. One manager I know writes to all his 100 per cent attenders once a year and says, simply: 'Thanks for making the effort.' Another way of thanking is to award, quietly and tactfully, a privilege or two. Extra time off, a meal for two, a bunch of flowers, a birthday present for a child, are all ways of recognizing someone's effort and/or achievement.

Reward, however, is a totally different matter. Reward will probably form part of the total remuneration package. So it may make sense to recognize this and be prepared to negotiate anything you want to *pay* for, over and above the norm.

It's also worth repeating the point made in Chapter 4, that rewarding performance is fraught with difficulties. By definition, performance-related pay will reward something *over and above* the normal call of duty. You already pay for job performance and should *reward* only when performance exceeds the standard.

It is essential to ensure that a basic performance management system exists in the first place. The following points should provide practical guidance.

Performance Management

1. Induction

We've already made reference to induction, but it must not be forgotten that it is a *key* first stage in managing performance.

What are the procedures for welcoming new employees? Do they work? Do they help newcomers settle quickly into your way of doing things? Do you make clear what you expect of them? How do you equip them to meet these expectations?

Induction is designed to help people settle into their jobs. Introduce them to the working environment and their colleagues, as well as making them aware of company policies and procedures. It acts as a solid foundation on which they can build.

Items to be included in an induction programme should include:

To whom am I responsible?
What exactly *is* my job?
With whom will I be working?
What standard is expected of me?
What training and support will I receive?
How will I be appraised, and by whom?

For the induction programme to work properly, good communication and co-ordination between personnel and line managers is critical.

2. Job descriptions

As soon as possible after joining the organization, a job description should be agreed with the newcomer. However, in reality too many job descriptions aren't even published let alone issued and too many more languish forgotten in desk drawers or personal files.

To what extent, therefore, do job descriptions help people understand what you want them to do, and to what standards?

A job description, apart from stating roles and responsibilities, should include standards of performance, normally identified within 6 to 8 key result areas. The relationship between the job description, standards of performance and targets, is shown in Figure 6 opposite.

Standards of performance
A standard of performance is a continuing yardstick covering about half a dozen key areas which will not change. It should judge whether *acceptable* performance is being achieved – not a pious hope, not perfection, but a realistic outcome with room for improvement.

Figure 6

The relationship between job description, standards of
performance and targets

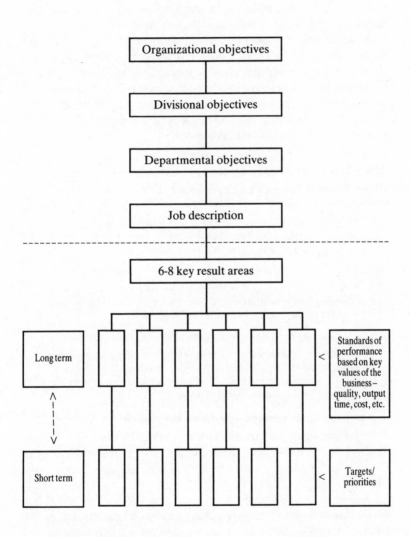

Standards of performance should include measurements such as:
    frequency
    averages
    percentages
    time limits
and be measurable in terms of quality, quantity and cost. They
should be reviewed annually or if the job changes.

Standards of performance may be easier to set in 'line' jobs such
as production or sales, this does not mean that they cannot (or
should not) be set in other types of work. They may require the co-
operation from colleagues in other departments to be fully realized.

In an ideal world, standards of performance are arrived at initially
by employees drafting their own ideas and bringing these to the
manager for discussion and agreement.

Examples of standards of performance
The following extracts illustrate what I mean.

A personnel manager in a department store, under the key area,
'external relations':

> 'All applications for employment are acknowledged by post
> within two days, and candidates are informed of the latest
> situation at intervals of not more than three weeks.'

A lecturer in a college under the key area 'student records':

> 'Student progress is formally reviewed on a termly basis at a
> meeting between staff member and student when the review
> report form is completed (see staff manual).'

An office manager under the key area 'staff communication':

> 'An office meeting is held at least once every ten working
> days at which local aims, achievements and action points are
> discussed and agreed upon. The meeting will have an agenda
> and will be minuted (see office manual).'

3. Managing improvement – performance review

The performance management process doesn't end with the job
description. You also need to review objectively the performance of
the job-holder against what you agreed with him or her in the first
place.

Does your organization have mechanisms for ensuring that
people know how well they're getting on – both individually, and as
a team? To what extent do these mechanisms actually work?

The aim of a review or appraisal scheme is to improve performance by:

- Assessing performance in the current job
- Identifying potential for development.

The performance interview

Good practice should include the following:

1. Clear agreement about how the interview will be conducted
2. Manager and employee should independently prepare for the interview by reviewing the individual's performance over the agreed time period
3. During the interview, the employee should explain how he or she feels they are getting on – his or her achievements and strengths, or weaknesses and areas for improvement
4. Agreement should be reached on performance in relation to baseline standards and targets/objectives (the emphasis should be on positive achievement)
5. Plans of action should be negotiated, and agreed upon
6. Arrangements set up for further monitoring.

4. Setting targets

The outcome of any successful performance review should be that the job-holder knows what *specifically* has to be achieved for performance to be improved. A vital part of this process is what has become known as 'setting targets'.

Do managers regularly set targets tailored to the individual? Do these targets develop the individual as well as meet the needs of the organization?

Targets are set by an individual's manager to:

- Bring performance up to an acceptable standard in the first place
- Return it to an acceptable level if performance has fallen below standard
- Stretch the individual beyond the basic acceptable standard.

As with standards of performance, targets need to be measurable in terms of quality, quantity, time and cost. But they are short-term and are likely to be set in relation to specific projects or responsibilities, or to encourage better performance on existing work.

Again, ideally, they are arrived at by the employee drafting out his or her own ideas and then bringing these to the manager for discussion.

Examples of targets:

'In your department over the next quarter, the attendance rate will be at least 96 per cent (excluding long-term illness).'

'Your error rate will drop by 4 per cent during the next 3 months.'

'By the end of the next month, increase the number of first-time customer visits from 20 to 25 per week.'

5. High fliers

Managing performance is about defining standards, reviewing achievement and setting targets in order to bridge the gap between what is being achieved and what is required. But what should you do with the individual who exceeds all expectations?

High fliers may represent only a small number of your workforce, say 5 per cent. But they are an important 5 per cent who will be the innovators, achievers and entrepreneurs. They will invariably be young, ambitious and will quickly become impatient with what they see as a bureaucratic system which holds them back. They'll want:

- recognition
- reward/better pay
- some idea of their career path
- careful, tactful encouragement.

You'll want to plan for their accommodation in a system that wasn't designed for them. You'll have to ensure that your pay and rewards systems are sufficiently flexible. And you will have to be prepared to explain openly any apparent inconsistencies. It all comes back to ensuring that there *is* a sound performance management system. Most people have an innate sense of fairness, so once they know and *accept* what the basic requirements and standards are, they'll recognize that someone who consistently exceeds them deserves some kind of exceptional treatment.

One note of warning however: *Not everyone can be a high flier. Don't cheat with the performance management system.* If you do, it will become corrupt and need replacing. I once knew a system which worked like this:

Category A: Outstanding
Category B: Average
Category C: Below average
Category D: Unacceptable

Nobody was ever allowed to be unacceptable.

Unacceptable people were marked C.

Below average people were marked B.

Average people were frequently marked A.

Outstanding people invariably left because they didn't want to be classified alongside people who struggled to keep pace with them.

Chapter 10
Managing Communication

A Few Principles

Employee communication is a function of *needs* rather than *wants*. It is more a matter of ensuring that people understand the necessities of the business and of working life than simply communicating what they want to hear. There is no checklist of topics which could be comprehensive enough to set out all the answers, although some generic headings are included here. A few working principles will help you define not only what to communicate but also the right order and the right style.

Communication should appeal to self-interest

Employees' interests start, understandably, with themselves and work upwards from this level to a point at which their interests coincide with those of the organization. For example, the individuals need to understand primarily what they are expected to do, what they will be paid, and how safe is their employment. After that, they become more interested in the contribution they make to the team and *vice versa*. On the other hand, the organization needs the employee to understand the basic requirements of the job, where it fits into the scheme of things, what the rewards will be and how other people depend on his or her contribution. Thus communication needs more or less coincide.

Communication should involve listening

Much experience, some of it very bitter, indicates how important it is to ensure that communication policies and practices provide for *listening* as well as *telling*. If people think that management is only interested in one-way communication, they will without doubt opt out. They may be very well behaved and civilized about it, but they will withdraw their interest, leaving at best their acquiescence.

A canning company was experiencing problems with the number of 'foreign bodies' that were the subject of customer complaints. These included stones and matchsticks (and other more unspeakable items) that ended up in cans of soup. The supervisor in charge of the vegetable sorting department decided to use a 'briefing' session to ask the women in his section for their views on the problem, only to be told that they understood it all too well. They had, in fact, already suggested a solution, based on rotating jobs, in order to reduce the boredom factor which caused them not to pick out the 'foreign bodies' by visual inspection. When the supervisor said he hadn't registered their interest before, they quoted him, chapter and verse, the occasions when they'd voiced their views! 'You never listen,' said one, 'and when you do, you don't take any notice.' Six months later, the 'foreign body' problem had been reduced by 50 per cent.

Communication should be regular and systematic

The fact that so many managers are associated with crisis or bad news is due to their propensity for only communicating at such times.

I asked a Higher Executive Officer in a Civil Service department how often he brought his team together for a meeting. 'About six times in the last three months,' he said. 'Mind you, we have had a lot of problems recently.' I then asked him how often he thought he *should* do it. 'Only when there's a problem.'

Yet people at work thrive upon and *need* communication – all the time. To disqualify them from it is simply to disqualify their potential.

Communication should be face-to-face, wherever possible

During the last 15 years the Employee Communication Audit has become a regular feature of employee relations or personnel policy. Every simple 'audit' which I have ever seen or conducted has confirmed that the single most important *need*, as expressed by work people in a confidential enquiry, is for face-to-face communication. They don't want just to read about the enterprise, they don't want just to see the Chief Executive on video, they overwhelmingly prefer to have the chance to listen and to ask questions. Without a policy that establishes face-to-face communication as the primary method, all the supporting investment in newspapers, magazines, notice boards, and videos is devalued.

Communication should be management-led

They may not always be very good at it, and they may not like it, but more than *two* out of every three people are emphatic that managers should explain themselves, answer questions, set out what is required and report on progress. In one factory survey, 60 per cent of employees said that their most frequent *actual* source of information was team room gossip; 80 per cent went on to say that their preferred source of information was the first-line manager.

Communication should be relevant to results

The whole purpose of investing time and money in the communication process is to enable employees and management jointly to reach an understanding of what has to be achieved and how it can all be made to happen in the most effective way. It has been said before that any business has its own series of core values. Communication, whatever else it is about, should be about those. People need to understand what the organization (and particularly their part of it) is *aiming* to do; they need to understand what is actually being *achieved*; and finally, they need to have the opportunity of discussing the *action* necessary to bridge the gap between aims and achievements. This can be set out in a simple diagram:

Figure 7

The Communication Grid

AIMS	Quality	Output	Time	Costs	Safety
ACHIEVEMENTS					
ACTION POINTS					

Once these needs are provided for, then by all means talk about anything else – pay, conditions, rewards, welfare, social activities etc. But it *starts* with the business because without the business there can *be* no pay, conditions, rewards etc.

Communication should be quality-linked

It isn't by accident that the first topic on the above 'grid' is 'quality'. The Japanese and the Germans have proved – as if it needed proving – that business success and quality are inextricably linked.

This isn't a book about Total Quality Management, but let me nail my colours to the mast. I am convinced from my own observation and experience that *everything* stems from 'getting it right first time'. I am, therefore, talking not about quality of product, but of method, environment, working life, working conditions. Identifying quality standards correctly at every stage will have the most profound effect on everything else. *Yet without workable and reliable communication policies, quality is inevitably undermined. At the same time, communication policies that don't provide for the discussion of quality simply won't work properly.*

Communication should be in teams

Team communication is crucial. Managing it is more difficult than it looks, so I have included some separate notes on this aspect of communication management (see Chapter 11). For the moment, let us just establish one or two basic points.

1. Team meetings aren't an optional extra. Direction and motivation *depend* on establishing and promoting a sense of common purpose – which means leader and team being united in trying to achieve commonly recognized business objectives

2. The effectiveness of team meetings is directly measurable on the bottom line. Since team meetings are about the core values of the business, you should be able to measure their effectiveness by examining the way results improve

3. Team meetings *are not* dependent on cascading a 'core brief' from the top of the organization and adding bits to it on the way. In my experience, such practices are of limited value, they invariably cause much irrelevant material to be aired at grassroots levels, and undermine commitment to the system.

   > In a major public utility, I was asked to audit the 'team briefing' system and recommend improvements. The system was based on the senior management 'core brief', sometimes known as 'the Yellow Pages', this being the colour of the document! The 'core brief' came once a month from the Board and was solemnly 'briefed' unaltered from level to level until it reached the bottom. Here it sank without trace. Criticism of the system was loud and bitter.

4. Team meetings should be two-way. Employees should be encouraged to ask questions and discuss the content of briefing sessions. How else is understanding to be achieved other than by question and answer?

Employee Communication Strategies

Employee communication isn't an *ad hoc* affair in which we preside over a pot pourri of: a company newspaper or two, a few team meetings and quality circles, a works council and so on. 'Well, of course not,' most personnel managers would say. Yet that's the reality for thousands of British companies which think they *ought* to do something about communication but haven't really worked out *how*.

The answer to the problem is to decide upon a *strategy*. This is a simple enough affair, a plan, linked to the organization's business objectives, setting out what needs to be communicated, by whom – and to whom.

Such a strategy should normally be based on the following assumptions:

- People would rather be winners than losers
- Employees who understand the aims and objectives of the organization are more likely to be supportive
- Organizational aims have to be converted into *operational plans* before they can be communicated by managers to employees (in other words, it's not good enough simply to communicate the budget and expect people to know what to do)
- Managers are responsible for making the connection between operational plans – and what these mean to the team and individuals
- Employee communication machinery and media are to support managers and must be focused constantly on the business
- *Positive communication should concentrate on the significance of events – and not their mere occurrence. Communication should look forward to and explain the reason for change – and not leave it to speculation.*

The key elements of an employee communication strategy

1. A written statement and guidelines demonstrate commitment (see the example below)
2. Management accountabilities should be publicly underlined
3. An annual plan shows how the principle issues and events are to be communicated – and by whom
4. Information priorities are identified in order to make available the data that needs to be understood

5. Management practice is developed and trained
6. Management of corporate/media channels ensures clarity and consistency between internal and external communications
7. Upward channels are developed
8. Training and development policies are updated
9. Tracking and monitoring are provided for.

Example of an employee communication policy: TESCO

In striving to achieve the company's aims, our Board recognizes the importance of everyone understanding what is expected of them, being aware of the Tesco way of doing things and appreciating the need for any changes which may be necessary.

To this end our Board intends:

1. That everyone in the company will be regularly informed about their own and the company's performance
2. That employees receive regular information about our business and changes within it which affect them
3. That managers and employees, at every level, regularly talk face-to-face about the needs of our business and those who work in it
4. That managers are regarded as personally accountable for the fair treatment of our employees, as well as our standards of service, quality and cost effectiveness, and that their performance in all these areas is regularly monitored
5. That we regularly measure the effectiveness of our communication policies whether with employees, customers, suppliers or shareholders.

Employee newspapers and bulletins

As *part* of an integrated employee communication strategy, employee newspapers have a relevant and valuable role. This checklist may help your organization make the most of them:

- Don't bombard employees with written information
- More people will read it if you keep it short; 'one-pagers' can be very valuable
- Get some advice on layout
- Use colour sparingly – two colours are better than one, but multicolour is not necessarily better than black and white
- Use simple language and short sentences and paragraphs

- Personalize as much as you can. (Avoid captions which say: 'Here is Sir John Bloggs our MD talking to a fitter')
- Print photos of people *doing* something. (Did you hear the story about the Chairman of a publicly quoted company who was nick-named 'Head and Shoulders' because some people said that was all they ever saw of him – framed on a video!)
- Avoid photos which are exclusively of senior executives at social events or inspecting the premises
- Ensure the bulk of content is *business- orientated*
- Don't be frightened of controversy – if you have a problem use your columns to share it with the readers
- Consult readers (employees) as much as you can.

Managing Communication with Supervisors

Unless your supervisors are an exception to the rule, they'll probably feel that communications are managed in such a way as to disenfranchise them. Here are a few ways to minimize their discomfort:

1. Ensure that team meeting policy is *strictly* implemented down to and including first-line management
2. Ensure that you invest as much time meeting supervisors as you do meeting shop stewards
3. Introduce a supervisors' bulletin
4. Run regular supervisors' conferences
5. Ensure supervisors sit on *all* representative committees at every level
6. Explore opportunities for maximizing supervisors' authority and enhancing their status.

Managing Communication with Shop Stewards or Employee Representatives

Ensure that you (and, more importantly, your line managers) meet shop stewards on a regular basis and in as positive a climate as possible. Do not talk to them only when either they or you have a problem! Talk regularly and don't be associated (or associate them) always with bad news or a crisis.

It's worth remembering that employee representatives don't often get thanked by their members (your employees) for their efforts. They don't get paid either. What they do get is endless questions. They are expected to know what's going on, to be able to handle grievances and complaints (yes, I know, so are supervisors) and to intercede on their constituents' behalf when an injustice is apparently being done. (I wouldn't be a shop steward for any reward.) They *don't* need to work in a climate in which they're starved of information and only see management on a 'needs must' basis.

Checklist

- See employee representatives *every day*
- Try to trust them
- Tell them as much as possible
- Help them to understand your business priorities
- Don't expect them to communicate your messages
- Remember, they're accountable to their members and not to management
- *Don't* tell your stewards or representatives *anything* without ensuring that you pass the same information to managers and supervisors
- Publish all meeting minutes *jointly*.

Chapter 11
Motivating the Team – Team Meetings

What Team Meetings Are

Nobody can hope to organize, manage and motivate a team without communicating effectively with it. The team meeting is the manager or supervisor's way of explaining the issues that employees *need* to understand.

The team meeting, in other words, is: a regular opportunity for *you* to talk with your own team, about the results for which *you* are accountable, and about the issues which will affect your and the team's ability to achieve them.

Team meetings are *not* simply a means of cascading information down the management line from top to bottom. (They work best when 'top down' information is kept to a minimum.) *Nor* are they negotiating meetings at which the pros and cons of decisions or policies are argued, although discussion and problem-solving should be the norm. *Nor* should they be a chore which has to be endured because somebody in senior management says so.

It is crucial that team meetings occur *regularly*; that means often enough for them to be a routine part of working life – not a major event. Monthly meetings are normally considered to be the most effective and should be diaried for the year. However, it often makes sense to hold team meetings more often.

The key principle of running team meetings is to *get the whole team together* and not rely on a series of one-to-one conversations.

What Should You Talk About?

People at work have a number of very basic communication requirements. They need to know about:

Aims: the goals which the team is trying for, in terms of quality, output, time or cost

Achievements: the actual level of achievement against the 'goals'

Action Points: what needs to be done to bridge the gap between aims and achievements.

The simple diagram below can be useful for recording these points:

Figure 8

KEY ISSUES	Quality	Output	Time	Cost
Aims				
Achievements				
Action Points				

There are a few basic rules about the *contents* of team meetings:
1. You should brief the aims and achievements before discussing the action points, so the meeting becomes a *two-way* affair
2. Once you've satisfied this requirement, you should add in any people issues, matters of local interest – and, of course, anything that's passed down from above by your boss
3. You'll probably find it helpful to agree the content of your meeting with your boss before you hold it
4. Take great care whenever you touch on controversial issues such as industrial-relations disputes, pay and conditions, etc. It is often a good idea to talk to your boss first.

How to Manage Team Meetings at Your Own Level

1. Decide on what is the best, or 'least worse', opportunity for bringing everybody together. Remember that it should be during working hours and as near the workplace as possible; convenience is probably more important than comfort. Early in the day is better than late
2. Decide how often, at least, they need to be held. The meeting is *your* affair, so you should manage it. Remember that less than once a month isn't likely to encourage the 'routine' approach, but be flexible about this – *don't* disrupt the business
3. Make sure everybody knows *where* and *when* meetings will take place

4. Meetings consist of the basic data you need to convey, any policy issues you are required to cover, and perhaps a ten-minute session answering questions (which you should attempt to anticipate). There should be no more than *7 or 8 minutes* worth of information altogether; meetings should probably last about half an hour

5. Remember it is your responsibility to find out the answer to any points/questions that you are not qualified/able to cope with. You will not be criticized for providing your team with the information it needs

6. Remember that even the simplest item can take you as much as 30 seconds to put over effectively.

Putting Over the Message

1. Use you own language and your own examples; you are the owner of the process!

2. Always use notes or you'll forget key points. Check you understand them before the meeting and try to anticipate likely questions and prepare suitable answers. On the other hand, avoid excessive paperwork and form-filling, so it doesn't all become too official

3. Stick to relevant subjects. Genuine 'feedback' is reaction to the message you are communicating or questions you are asked but couldn't answer! (You may also, however, have to make separate arrangements to listen to the team's complaints, worries, grumbles and groans. If you don't, you could be there all day!)

4. Use visual aids wherever you can; flip charts, blackboards etc are always helpful

5. Get the group tightly organized – don't have people sitting in odd corners, etc.

6. Get someone to man the phone

7. Don't try to handle too many people at once. If the team is very large (over 20), split it into two and repeat the exercise

8. If you're concerned about your ability to control discussion or handle 'difficult' team members, discuss this with your boss

9. Keep your notes in a safe place.

Measuring the Effectiveness of Team Meetings

Since you are investing your time in talking to the team, you ought to be interested in ensuring that you achieve a return on that investment.

1. Feed into the system issues which you can reasonably expect to improve measurably as a result of a reminder, (quality, customer care, timekeeping, attendance, cost control, output etc)
2. Check that employees actually understood what you told them and that they are *doing something* as a result
3. Ask employees if there are issues that they need to understand more about
4. If you're a senior manager, talk to employees informally, in order to check that they actually understand what they *need* to understand
5. Supervisors and their immediate managers should regularly discuss the effectiveness of team meetings
6. It can be a very good idea for senior managers to 'sit in' on meetings occasionally.

Key Management Responsibilities

First-line managers/supervisors are the prime communicators. Most of the messages should start at this level, but should be agreed in advance with

Second-line managers, who should be accountable for support, coaching, answering questions and being the link with

Senior managers/executives, whose job it is to ensure that meetings are a regular feature of company policy and employment strategy, and not some kind of optional extra.

Since managers 'own' the process, it makes sense to ensure that there are agreed objectives and targets at every level. These are fundamental to the team's ability to make its most effective contribution.

If the teams don't know where the goals are – and whether they are scoring any – they very quickly stop trying. It is ultimately senior management's responsibility to ensure that:

- Everyone knows what is expected and needed
- Everyone is consulted about goals
- Everyone is regularly told about progress.

Team meetings are the most simple – and the most effective – way of achieving such objectives.

Team Meetings and Trade Unions

Just as trade union representatives claim, and should be given, the right to discuss trade union matters with their members, managers have both a right and a duty to discuss their business with their employees (ie the same people). Unions will not oppose team meetings unless you use them for communicating propaganda or a distorted picture of management/union activities (eg *your* views about *their* pay claim!). Courtesy suggests that you should always keep representatives informed about content.

Management/union relations will not be helped by anyone getting into a series of exchanges on the lines of 'Oh yes, we did', 'Oh no, you didn't.' If you can't agree your business with trade union representatives it is only as a very last resort that you should try and use team meetings as a means of winning hearts as well as minds. Yet remember that employees who are union members have union as well as company loyalties. The way to achieve employee support is by helping them to understand as much as possible about the business. Then they're much more likely to take actions which serve corporate objectives.

Chapter 12
Making Motivation Happen

Everything which I've recommended in this book is based on practical experience. It *will* work, and work well, provided you do things in the right order and in the right way. This chapter sets out a few underlying principles to help you manage the process of 'turning people on'.

1. Leadership

Projects need champions – and motivation at work is the most important thing about competitiveness, cost-effectiveness – or simply staying alive – is the commitment and application of people at work. But it all depends on leadership. Here, therefore, are a few guidelines:

- *Practise what you preach* – whatever you're recommending, ensure that *you* already do it! Someone will undoubtedly ask you

- *Talk to the man or woman at the top* – ensure that your words of wisdom or advice are always directed at the person who can press the 'go' button

- *Find positive reasons for promoting change* – in other words, always stress the potential benefits, rather than the penalties

- *Show/demonstrate/explain/enthuse* – instead of writing memos, pamphlets, papers or dissertations, go and talk to people. Get the manager concerned together with his team and talk to them about your ideas.

2. Surveys

Changing behaviour, and hence, attitudes, is difficult unless you can identify a start point. Some of your colleagues, who will much prefer to preserve current values and resist change will want to know *why* you wish to change their world. So defining what the problem is and why it exists, is of crucial importance, and a simple objective survey often helps. Here are some basic principles:

- Stay away from quantitative audits that require people to fill in questionnaires. Such exercises need specialist design and analysis

- Concentrate on qualitative exercises instead. Seek facts, opinions, quotes from employees. Compare or contrast what happens – with what *should* happen

- Look for positive examples of behaviour on which to report. I once discovered much more about labour turnover by asking people why they *stayed* with the organization than by ploughing remorselessly through piles of exit interviews

- Don't risk 'paralysis by analysis'! In other words, don't analyse the problems to death. Far better to gather chapter and verse, *working to pre-defined terms of reference*. You can then help your colleagues to reach conclusions and draw up action plans, *based on established good practice* either in your own organization or elsewhere

- Report quickly, briefly and objectively. Don't make sweeping statements and discuss your conclusions early with the key players

- Give everyone who took part a copy – at least of your recommendations

- Don't recommend too much change. People can only cope with so much at any one time. I've experienced many occasions when I frightened my client by presenting them with a chapter of indictments which simply prompted the response: 'We can't be that bad.'

3. Making Use of Good Practice

I've lost count of the number of people who, over the years, have asked questions like: 'Can you train managers in leadership skills?', 'Can you set objectives for this or that kind of job?', 'Do performance review systems actually *work*?', 'Do briefing systems or team meetings pay off?'

The answer is: of course these things work, and of course they pay off. However, 'home-grown' versions of them work better than textbook methods. The 'trick' is to take a concept, read the theory –

and then throw away the textbook! Visit a few organizations which already implement whatever it is you're considering, learn from their successes or failures, and then *adapt* the technique or practice to your own organization.

4. Pilot Schemes

Pilot schemes are sometimes useful for controlled experiments with established techniques. As a general rule, if it hasn't been tried and found to work elsewhere, don't experiment with it in your organization. *You don't have that right.*

5. No Panaceas

There is no such thing in motivation as the Holy Grail. Nor should you believe in magic. When management consultants come along and tell you they've discovered the universal cure-all, treat them like the confidence tricksters they are.

6. Human Resource Strategy

There should be one – a paper which sets out the human 'values' of the organization. Such a stategy should be relevant to corporate objectives and set out what the organization believes in. If, for example, it is committed to values such as:

> delegating accountability to the lowest level
> team work
> harmonized conditions of employment
> performance review for all
> two-way face-to-face communication
> a positive approach towards trade union activity,

– or whatever – then there should be a strategy document which provides for these things to happen in a relevant way.

7. Policies and Procedures

Nothing ever happens unless there's a simple policy or procedure for *making it happen*. It should set out:

> what should take place
> who should manage it
> how it should happen
> how it will be monitored.

This may seem very obvious, but have you checked recently to make sure the necessary procedures *actually exist?* And more important still, have they been *communicated?*

8. Tackle the Roadblocks

If you're confronted by a manager who doesn't implement what is agreed and required, *take it seriously*! Talk to him or her, try to ascertain whether you're dealing with an issue of *conduct* (ie they *won't* play ball) or capability (ie they *can't*) – then decide whether it is a question of training, counselling or talking to their boss. Don't fudge the issue and hope it will go away.

9. Be an Idealist

Changing part of the world isn't a bad thing to want to do. Just try not to be boring about it! And remember that enthusiasm counts and is infectious. (It has been earning me a living for over 20 years.)

10. Keep it Simple

Managers are busy people, complex people, technical or financial people – and invariably *ordinary* people. They do *not* need nor respond to complex psychological models or theories. If you're into Transactional Analysis, Neuro-Linguistic Programming, Continuums of Behaviour, Managerial Grids, Circles, Squares or other exercises in management geometry – *translate them into usable English.*

11. Be Positive

Nothing – absolutely nothing – is as bad as a cynical personnel manager who can't resist telling colleagues why nothing works, and why nothing else is worth trying. If you don't think that turning people on is part of the job or a valuable and important initiative, what else do you think matters more? Should you be in this role? Would you perhaps be better suited to a more solitary occupation?

Very few people will prevent you from implementing at least some of the ideas in this book, provided you go about it in the right way. If you ask permission, however, you may get a 'wait and see' response, mainly because whoever it was you talked to simply doesn't know as much about the proposed initiative as you. Always frame your ideas as proposals:

> start with the benefits
> follow up with the method
> explain the investment required
> go back to the benefits.

It isn't selling – it's just commonsense.